the
WORD
& You

the
WORD
& You

United Church Press
Cleveland, Ohio

A Lectionary-based Exploration of the Bible

Volume 2 (From Proper 17, Year C, to Proper 16, Year A)

Edited by Nan Duerling

United Church Press, Cleveland, Ohio 44115
© 1998 by United Church Press

03 02 01 00 99 98   5 4 3 2 1

Library of Congress Cataloging-in-Publication Data

The Word and you : a lectionary-based exploration of the Bible /
      edited by Nan Duerling
         p.   cm.
      Includes index
      Contents: v. 1, From proper 18, year B, to proper 16, year C.
      ISBN 0-8298-1165-6 (alk. paper)
      1. Bible—Study and teaching. 2. Common lectionary (1992)—Study and
teaching I. Duerling, Nan.
BS600.2.W67 1997
264'.34—DC21   97-16314
                                                                       CIP

Volume 2, ISBN 0-8298-1241-5

Contents

An Invitation into the Word

Welcome to an exciting spiritual and biblical journey through the church year with *The Word and You: A Lectionary-based Exploration of the Bible*. This resource, which is organized around readings from *The Revised Common Lectionary*, will help you to explore the Scriptures using a systematic plan that includes the seasons and festivals throughout the Christian calendar. Many find that the use of the lectionary gives vitality and focus to corporate worship while strengthening one's understanding and response to the Bible's claim upon one's life.

The Word and You is a scripture-centered study designed to deepen and broaden your spiritual life through engagement with the stories and teachings of the Bible. Some art, lyrics, and literature are included in this volume to enrich your experience of God's presence in your life, in your faith community, and in all creation. Your encounter with the Word of God may spark questions, evoke prayers, inspire individual and corporate responses, and motivate new or renewed commitments. Our hope is that you will be nurtured and challenged by the written Word so that it may become the living Word that guides your daily journey of faith.

Using *The Word and You*

The Word and You may be used in a variety of settings. Some
readers will use it as a guide for independent study. Adult Bible
study groups that meet on Sunday morning or during the week may
choose it for their text. If you participate in such a group, you will
have the benefit of exchanging ideas and insights with other members of the community of faith. Some of these groups may also be
using the adult learner's and leader's guides of *The Inviting Word*, a
curriculum that encompasses all age levels so that everyone in the
congregation experiences the same lectionary passage on a particular Sunday.

Since *The Word and You* is based on the lectionary, which is the
centerpiece of worship in many congregations, the lesson progresses
in much the same way as a worship service does as learners enter
the Word, engage the Word, respond to the Word, and go with the
Word.

- In the upper right corner you will notice the liturgical date
  and calendar dates to designate the week for which a particular reading is appropriate. These dates correspond to the
  church calendar as set forth in the *Revised Common
  Lectionary*, a three-year cycle (years A, B, and C) of readings used in churches of many denominations as the focus
  of preaching and worship. The readings generally include a
  passage from the Hebrew Scriptures (Old Testament),
  Psalms, Gospels, and Epistles or other New Testament writings. During the season following Pentecost (ordinary
  time), which varies in length depending upon when Easter
  occurs, the lectionary readings are numbered as Propers.
  The current volume of *The Word and You* runs from Proper

17 of Year C through Proper 16 of Year A. A prior volume and a subsequent volume of *The Word and You* complete the lectionary cycles.

- Under the title, you will find a verse or two of scripture that contains the core of the theme for the week.
- The scripture designated as the "Bible Reading" is the main text of the lesson.
- The "Additional Bible Readings" include the rest of the lectionary readings for the week.
- "Enter the Word" includes two bulleted questions, along with suggestions to help you think about the ideas in the Bible reading as it relates to your own life. A prayer is offered at the close of this portion.
- "Engage the Word" opens with a question that will encourage you to consider how the original hearers of this text might have understood it centuries ago and the impact that the text could have had on their faith journeys. The passage that follows the question, written by biblical scholars Dr. Paul Hammer and Dr. Clarice Martin, provides you with background that sets the passage in its context and explores its implications for the original audience and for contemporary Christians as well.
- "Respond to the Word" challenges you to take actions and make commitments that enable the text to live through you and possibly your faith community.
- "Go with the Word" provides a prayer, lyrics, poem, other literary excerpt, or art to activate your imagination so that your head and heart will unite in this study of God's Word.

As each new season of the church year begins, you will find an overview of the season's place in the church year, its dominant color, and an art selection that captures its significance. As you begin this study, you may want to read all of the seasonal dividers for Pentecost (the end of Year C), Advent, Christmas, Epiphany, Lent, Easter, and Pentecost (the beginning of Year A) to get a panoramic sweep of the entire Christian year.

However you choose to use this book, we pray that you will be touched by the presence of the living, loving, forgiving God in your life, for in that is the real purpose of any Bible study.

Rick Reinhard, *Laying on of Hands*, Washington, D.C.
© Rick Reinhard/Impact Visuals. Used by permission.

Pentecost

Seven weeks after the first Easter, Jews gathered in Jerusalem to celebrate Pentecost, the traditional festival of gratitude for the harvest. On that day God poured out the Holy Spirit upon Jesus' disciples and the Christian church was born. The season of Pentecost, known as ordinary time, begins the day after Pentecost and continues to the end of November when Advent begins.

During this longest season of the church year the gospel readings focus on the stories and teachings of Jesus. Through parables— those stories rooted in familiar people, places, and things—Jesus confronts his hearers with what it means to participate in the reign of God. Jesus' interactions with seekers, followers, and opponents point the way for disciples to live out the call of Christ upon their lives. Spiritual growth, which occurs in the ordinariness of our daily work, play, and worship, is nurtured by recollections of Jesus' life and teachings. The liturgical color of this season, fittingly, is green, a reminder of abundant life and growth.

Look at the photograph *Laying on of Hands*. Ponder your own commitment to Christ. Pray that God will give you the wisdom and grace to grow toward more faithful discipleship.

Invite the Forgotten

Jesus said also to the person who had invited him,

"When you give a luncheon or a dinner, do not invite

your friends or your brother or sister or your relatives or

rich neighbors, in case they may invite you in return,

and you would be repaid. But when you give a banquet,

invite those who are poor, crippled, lame, and blind.

Luke 14:12–13

Bible Reading: Luke 14:1, 7–14

Additional Bible Readings: Jeremiah 2:4–13/Psalm 81:1, 10–16
or Proverbs 25:6–7/Psalm 112
Hebrews 13:1–8, 15–16

Enter the Word

- How have you felt when you were not invited to an event you particularly wanted to attend?
- To whom does God issue invitations?

Recall how it feels to be invited to attend special events and parties. Contrast those feelings with what it would be like to be forgotten or excluded from a celebration only because the host thought that he or she had little to gain from your presence. Keep these feelings in mind as you read Luke 14:1, 7–14.

Imagine yourself in each role portrayed in the reading. First, envision the host asking you to move from a seat of honor that you had selected. Experience your feelings in such an awkward situation. Next, think about how you would feel if you were the host and had to ask someone to move. You may feel awkward, too, but you had a place reserved for a special guest that someone else took without asking. Finally, consider how you would react if you were invited to a dinner that you never expected to attend, such as a presidential inaugural party.

As you study the additional readings for the day note the way God and humans are depicted by the writers. Ponder the hospitality that you offer to God and the extent to which you include the marginalized people of the world in your life.

> *Gracious God, you invite each of us to your banquet feast. Help me to extend hospitality to all, especially to those who are often forgotten. Amen.*

Engage the Word

- What insights about God's hospitality might Luke's Gentile readers have garnered from Jesus' teaching?

Luke had a passion for proclaiming God's inclusiveness. He wanted his community toward the end of the first century to know and proclaim that God's "good news of great joy" in Jesus' coming was for all people (Luke 2:10). He proclaimed that this good news was for persons whom society and even the religious community often marginalized and rejected as outcasts.

As Luke tells the story, that good news reached out to outcast shepherds at the beginning and to a criminal crucified with Jesus at the end. It reached out to despised tax collectors and Samaritans, even to the Roman soldiers who crucified Jesus. It reached out to the put-down women and children, to the poor, and to persons who were physically and mentally challenged.

For Luke, as Jesus announced his Spirit-empowered mission by quoting from the prophet Isaiah, that mission included persons who were poor, captive, without sight, and oppressed (4:18–19). And when John the Baptist wondered whether Jesus really was the Messiah, Jesus pointed to what he was doing for the diseased and those possessed by evil spirits, for those with physical disabilities, for the dead and the poor (7:21–22). Today's passage focuses on hospitality for the poor, the crippled, the lame, the blind (14:13).

This scripture is part of a larger section in Luke on God's healing and hospitality. At a dinner party Jesus challenged prevailing rules about the Sabbath to bring God's healing to a person with dropsy (14:1–6). Next he told a parable to challenge the way people chose the honored seats at a marriage feast (14:7–11). Then he instructed his host on whom to invite to a luncheon or dinner (14:12–14).

The guests were not to be relatives or rich neighbors who can invite you back. That is not God's way. In God's reign, the poor and those with disabilities, persons forgotten and even rejected are to be invited to fellowship at the table. The religious elite ostracized these marginalized persons because the elite perceived their poverty and disability to be the result of sin.

But God's reign is the way of compassion and outreach to such hurting persons. They belong at the table and those who invite them are the truly "righteous" whom God will reward at the future resurrection (14:14). The righteous are the compassionate.

Here Luke provided another example of Jesus' breaking barriers to proclaim the nature of God's hospitality, a hospitality to which Jesus calls his followers. They are to show it at their own dinner tables. Those tables then make real in human homes God's great caring for all people in Jesus, a caring celebrated at the communion table. Their tables extend the communion table.

The epistle reading for today also speaks of love and hospitality. "Let mutual love continue. Do not neglect to show hospitality to strangers, for by doing that some have entertained angels without knowing it" (Hebrews 13:1–2).

Respond to the Word

- What groups do you, or could you, work with in order to demonstrate God's hospitality to those who are often forgotten?
- What specific action can you take this week on behalf of one who needs to experience God's inclusive love in a tangible way?

Go with the Word

Feast of Life

> *Come on.*
> *Let us celebrate the supper of the Lord.*
> *Let us make a huge loaf of bread*
> *and let us bring abundant wine like at the*
> *wedding at Cana.*
>
> *Let the women not forget the salt.*
> *Let the men bring along the yeast.*
> *Let many guests come,*
> *the lame, the blind, the crippled, the poor.*
>
> *Come quickly.*
> *Let us follow the recipe of the Lord.*
> *All of us, let us knead the dough together*
> *with our hands.*
> *Let us see with joy how the bread grows.*
>
> *Because today*
> *we celebrate*
> *the meeting with the Lord.*
> *Today we renew our commitment*
> *to the kingdom.*
> *Nobody will stay hungry.*

Elsa Tamez, "Feast of Life," in *International Review of Mission*, 1982.

Fearfully and Wonderfully Made

I praise you, for I am fearfully and wonderfully made.

Psalm 139:14a

Bible Reading: Psalm 139:1–6, 13–18

Additional Bible Readings: Jeremiah 18:1–11
or Deuteronomy 30:15–20/Psalm 1
Philemon 1–21
Luke 14:25–33

Enter the Word

- What does the title of the lesson, quoted from Psalm 139:14, suggest to you about God's relationship with and concern for humanity?
- How do you perceive yourself to be a unique creation of God, gifted and wonderfully made?

Each day this week, read Psalm 139:1–6 and 13–18 aloud. Let the scripture speak to you personally. Sit still and be aware of your body. Observe your breathing and let it calm down. Let your muscles relax. Try to rid yourself of stress.

Consider ways in which your body, mind, and self make you a unique individual. Ponder how your uniqueness connects to Psalm 139. Identify particular skills and talents you have that are gifts from God. Also assess your care for the body, mind, and emotional life that God has given you. One way of praising God is by caring for the gifts of God, including your body and mind.

Be alert for relationships between Psalm 139 and the additional Bible readings. Each one celebrates God's people in some way. In Jeremiah 18:1–11 God is portrayed fashioning humanity as a potter molds clay. Contemplate how this image reinforces the idea that humans are wonderfully made. Psalm 1 contrasts the righteous ones who obey God's word with the evildoers who ignore it. Deuteronomy 30:15–20 also speaks of two ways of life and stipulates that God's people must decide which way they will choose. Philemon 1–21 appeals to the transforming, forgiving love that exists within the church. In Luke 14:25-33 Jesus helps his listeners understand that God must be the first priority of all who would be his disciples.

> *Thanks and praise to you, O God, for I am a unique individual wonderfully made by your creating hand. Amen.*

Engage the Word

- How does Psalm 139 help readers to recognize their intimate connection with the all-knowing God?

Psalms or parts of them often take the form of hymnic prayer in the worship life of Israel. Written as poetry, the whole of Psalm 139 is one such prayer.

Composed and used over several centuries, Psalms became Israel's song and prayer book. It reflects the whole spectrum of human experience: from praise and thanksgiving to despair and death, from pleading innocence to crying out for revenge against one's enemies.

Psalm 139 is a prayer in which a person, falsely accused, pleads innocence on the basis of God's knowledge of that person. It begins with the words, "O God, you have searched me and known me" (Psalm 139:1). It ends with "Search me, O God, and know my heart; test me and know my thoughts. See if there is any wicked way in me, and lead me in the way everlasting" (139:23–24). Though a person may see herself or himself as innocent, God is the final judge and the One who can search and lead to new paths of life.

The psalm has four parts (139:1–6, 7–12, 13–18, 19–24), though today's reading from Psalm 139:1–6 and 13–18 includes only the first and third. Part one focuses on God's current knowledge of a person; part two on the impossibility of ever escaping from God; part three on God the Creator's total knowledge of all persons even before their birth. Part four calls for the end of the malicious accusers, sides with God against God's enemies, and concludes with "search me" (139:23–24).

In part one the psalmist prays that God knows both a person's passive and active life: sitting down and rising up (139:2). God knows the person's thoughts (139:2). God knows the person's daily walk, sleeping, everything he or she does (139:3), even the person's words before they are spoken (139:4). God surrounds the person (139:5). For the psalmist, God's knowledge is overwhelming (139:6).

After declaring that there is no escape from God (139:7–12), in part three the psalmist acknowledges that God is the all-knowing Creator. God has formed the psalmist from the womb (139:13). At this point the psalmist then praises God, "for I am fearfully and wonderfully made," as are all of God's works (139:14). God knew the psalmist in the secret embryonic process, when life's substance was yet unformed, and the psalmist's future days were in God's book before any of them ever happened (139:15–16).

Again the psalmist is overwhelmed by the vastness of God's thoughts (Psalm 139:17–18). Yet the amazing thing is that after all this affirmation of God's vast knowledge, the psalmist could pray, "I am still with you" (139:18). The great Creator and Knower of all things is not some far-removed impersonal power. The mighty God is personally present to the psalmist.

As God's creation, we are fearfully (i.e., awe-fully) and wonderfully made, and the awesome and wonderful Creator is with us as we pray to this searching, leading, everlasting God.

Respond to the Word

- What steps can you take to transform a difficult relationship by honoring the other person as a wonderfully made creation of God?
- What commitment will you make this week to take better care of your body? Consider options such as healthier eating habits, regular exercise, a physical exam, or breaking harmful habits.

Go with the Word

Grandfather took us out
long after dark
and set his telescope up on the lawn
and showed us how to look through the lens.
We saw the mountains of the moon!
We saw the rings around Saturn!
We saw the stars in the Milky Way—
too many to count!
"See," Grandfather said,
"what wonders God has made!"
And then he hugged each one of us
and said, "And you are wondrous, too!"

Madeleine L'Engle, *Anytime Prayers* (Wheaton, Ill: Harold Shaw, 1994), 52. © Crosswicks, 1994. Used by permission of Harold Shaw Publishers, Wheaton IL 60189.

Seek, Find, Rejoice

When the woman has found the coin, she calls together her friends and neighbors, saying, "Rejoice with me, for I have found the coin that I had lost."

Luke 15:9

Bible Reading: Luke 15:1–10

Additional Bible Readings: Jeremiah 4:11–12, 22–28/Psalm 14
or Exodus 32:7–14/Psalm 51:1–10
1 Timothy 1:12–17

Enter the Word

- When have you rejoiced over finding that which was lost?
- How has God sought you out?

As you read Luke 15:1–10, think of yourself as one of the lost who is being sought. Then think of yourself as one who is seeking the lost. Perhaps you can envision yourself as the woman in Vuillard's *Sweeping Woman* pictured at the end of this lesson. Discern different reasons for rejoicing as you consider Luke 15:1–10 from these different perspectives.

As you reflect on this lesson, think of ways you have felt lost from God. Recall what led you astray. Recollect how you felt when you recognized that you were lost. Remember who or what helped you back to the fold.

As you read 1 Timothy 1:12–17 notice how the writer confesses with thanksgiving and humility how he was lost and led back to God's grace. Consider the impact of such grace on one's ability to serve and minister unto others.

Another additional reading, Exodus 32:7–14, shows how, through Moses, God continued to seek the hearts and minds of people who had turned away so that they might be restored. The writer of Psalm 14 laments that the people have perversely strayed from God. Jeremiah 4:11–12 and 22–28 speaks of Judah's impending defeat, for these people have also strayed from God. In Psalm 51:1–10, the psalmist recognizes that he needs to be restored to God.

These passages remind us that we can't write off some people as hopelessly lost. The coin in Luke 15 didn't lose itself. The parable focuses, not on whether the lost deserve their condition, but on God's intent for all creation to be united.

> *God, I lift up one who is lost. Empower me to work with you to seek that dear one so that he or she might find you. Then let us rejoice together. Amen.*

Engage the Word

- How would the original hearers of this parable, the outcasts of society, on the one hand, and the pious, on the other, have responded to Jesus' message?

Parables were a major form of Jesus' verbal communication. He took images close to the daily life of his hearers and wove them into stories. These parable-stories were intended to confront his hearers with aspects of their lives and to call them to decision.

Some of the most famous of Jesus' parables are in the Gospel of Luke. The parable of the good Samaritan confronted his hearers with a decision about loving one's neighbor by being a neighbor. The parable of the Pharisee and tax collector in the Temple confronted Jesus' hearers with a decision about humility (as did the parable from Luke 14 in Proper 18).

The parable of the lost son (which follows today's highlighted verses in Luke 15) confronted Jesus' hearers with a decision about "lost" persons. This parable and the two parables in the highlighted verses all have to do with what is lost and with an appropriate response to finding what is lost.

Who is the audience for these parables? Who are the hearers being confronted? There are two sets: the tax collectors and sin-

ners, on the one hand, the Pharisees and scribes, on the other—
outcasts of society and the most respected religious people (Luke
15:1–2). The latter objected to Jesus' eating with and welcoming
the former (15:2). Jesus included. They excluded.

In the two parables of the lost sheep and the lost coin, Luke
followed a pattern he repeats elsewhere. He includes a text with a
male character followed by a text with a female character: here a
seeking shepherd and a seeking woman. It was one way that Luke
balanced the place of men and women in his story of Jesus.

When the outcast tax collectors (collaborators with Rome) and
sinners (i.e., those who did not live up to the rules of the religious
authorities) heard of the lost sheep and the lost coin, would they
see themselves as lost and sought by the seeking God?

When the religious Pharisees and scribes heard of the found
sheep and recovered coin, would they continue to object to Jesus'
eating and welcoming sinners? Or would they too repent, change
their minds, break down barriers, and enter into the heavenly joy of
God's angels?

The parables place great emphasis on the single sheep among a
hundred and the single coin among ten. Ninety-nine percent is
good; ninety percent is good too. Why bother with the one percent
or ten percent that is "lost"? Jesus teaches that God does not deal
in percentages. Instead, God cares for every single person and treasures every single one.

Jesus did not want tax collectors and sinners to be separated
from Pharisees and scribes. He wanted all at God's party. So did
Luke sixty years later. He wanted joy in God's one human family.

Respond to the Word

- How can you, perhaps working with your church or another group, seek others whom society labels as the lost, the
  outcast?
- How will you welcome a newcomer to the Christian faith?

Go with the Word

Édouard Vuillard, *Woman Sweeping*, ca. 1899–1900, The Phillips
Collection, Washington, D.C. Used by permission.

Grieve with God

Hark, the cry of my poor people from far and wide in the land: "Is God not in Zion? Is Zion's Ruler not there?" (Why have they provoked me to anger with their images, with their foreign idols?)

Jeremiah 8:19

Bible Reading:	Jeremiah 8:18–9:1
Additional Bible Readings:	Psalm 79:1–9 or Amos 8:4–7/Psalm 113 1 Timothy 2:1–7 Luke 16:1–13

Enter the Word

- What situations do you believe cause God to grieve today?
- How do you grieve with God?

What is your image of God? The prophet Jeremiah often described God as having the same traits as that of a parent. Read Jeremiah 8:18–9:1. Through this poetic passage, the prophet shows his grief for the people. God is grieving too. Like a parent, God cares deeply about the people and grieves when they do not behave in the ways God expects. God is sometimes overcome with emotion at the choices and decisions of God's people. Recall an experience when you grieved because of the self-destructive actions of someone close to you.

In addition to our personal grief, the pain and suffering in the world causes us to grieve with God as Jeremiah did. Even if we aren't called away from our own sphere of existence, images from the media make us aware of this suffering. Remember some news images showing how innocent children are starving, orphaned, and dying *en masse* as a direct result of political strife or natural catastrophe. In response, we might indeed utter the prophet's words in Jeremiah 9:1, willing to weep for those who are hurting. Lift your personal pain and the anguish you feel over the pain in the world to God.

Continue your study by reading the lament in Psalm 79:1–9 and the hymn of celebration unto God, helper of the humble, in Psalm 113. Read the scathing words against those who exploit the poor in Amos 8:4–7. First Timothy 2:1–7 proclaims that God's grace is available to all. Luke 16:1–13 recounts Jesus' parable of the dishonest manager or steward.

> *Compassionate God, empower me to be a balm for those*
> *in pain that they might know of your love for them.*
> *Amen.*

Engage the Word

- How does Jeremiah, who prophesied before and during the fall of Jerusalem, embody and express the grief of God?

The prophet Jeremiah lived some six hundred years before Jesus came. He was active as a prophet for about forty years until the fall of Jerusalem and the beginning of the exile of many of his people in Babylon in 587 B.C.E. (Note Psalm 79.)

He involved himself deeply in political affairs and often found himself in conflict with government leaders. The word "prophet" means one who "speaks for" God; and to speak for God's justice and truth and integrity in the midst of injustice and lies and corruption can land one in trouble. It did Jeremiah.

Jeremiah 8:18–9:1 depicts his awful anguish and grief over the state of affairs of his people. For a broader context of his grief, also read Jeremiah 8:1–17 and 9:2–11.

Jeremiah interpreted the sorry state of his people as the result of their disobedience: "Everyone is greedy for unjust gain; from prophet to priest everyone deals falsely. They have treated the wound of my people carelessly, saying 'Peace, peace,' when there is no peace" (8:10–11); "for the Sovereign our God has doomed us to perish . . . because we have sinned against God" (8:14).

But Jeremiah was not a prophet who could rejoice over the doom that he saw coming. No, he said, "My joy is gone, grief is upon me, my heart is sick" (8:18).

The poor, who suffered from the greed, lies, oppression, and deceit, cried out for God. "Is God not in Zion? Is Zion's Ruler not there?" (8:19; this verse points also to images and foreign idols as provoking God's anger). The cry of the poor continued, "The harvest is past, the summer is ended, and we are not saved" (8:20). They have not been saved from hunger; their economic needs have not been met.

Jeremiah then asserted, "For the hurt of my poor people I am hurt, I mourn, and dismay has taken hold of me" (8:21). He went on to speak about the need for balm, a physician, and restoration of the health of poor people (8:22). Jeremiah cried out for economic justice and health care for the poor.

He expressed the depth and poetic power of his anguish: "O that my head were a spring of water, and my eyes a fountain of tears, so that I might weep day and night for the slain of my poor people!" (9:1). He anguishes deeply over the pain of others.

Jeremiah then indicates that he would like to run away from it all: "O that I had in the desert a traveler's lodging place, that I might leave my people and go away from them!" (9:2).

But the cries of Jeremiah were not only his. God spoke through Jeremiah's words (note "says the Lord" in Jeremiah 8:17; 9:3). God's joy was gone too; God grieved; God's heart was sick; God wept for the poor. But neither God nor Jeremiah left the people. They kept prophesying, speaking God's truth.

Respond to the Word

- What situations in your own community can you and your group address so as to bring healing to those who suffer?
- Whose pain can you help to alleviate? How will you do that?

Go with the Word

There Is a Balm in Gilead

There is a balm in Gilead, to make the wounded whole,
there is a balm in Gilead, to heal the sinsick soul.

Sometimes I feel discouraged, and think my work's in vain,
But then the Holy Spirit revives my soul again.

Don't ever feel discouraged, for Jesus is your friend,
who, if you ask for knowledge, will never fail to lend.

If you cannot preach like Peter, if you cannot pray like Paul,
you can tell the love of Jesus, who died to save us all.

African American spiritual, in *The New Century Hymnal* (Cleveland,
Ohio: The Pilgrim Press, 1995), 553, alt. Used by permission.

The Way of Faith

Pursue righteousness, godliness, faith, love, endurance, gentleness. Fight the good fight of the faith; take hold of the eternal life, to which you were called.

1 Timothy 6:11b–12a

Bible Reading: 1 Timothy 6:6–19

Additional Bible Readings: Jeremiah 32:1–3a, 6–15/
    Psalm 91:1–6, 14–16
    or Amos 6:1a, 4–7/Psalm 146
    Luke 16:19–31

Enter the Word

- How would you describe the way of faith?
- What are you doing—and what do you want to be doing—to live out your faith?

First Timothy provides direction as to what our goals should be as faithful followers of Christ. It urges us to "pursue righteousness, godliness, faith, love, endurance, gentleness" (1 Timothy 6:11). It also encourages us to "fight the good fight of the faith" (6:12). And it explains how we are to accomplish all of this: "do good . . . be rich in good works, generous, and ready to share" (6:18).

As you read 1 Timothy 6:6–19, ponder some of the choices you have made in life and how they did or did not reflect your faith. Identify portions of the text that make you feel uneasy as you consider your own discipleship. Pinpoint specific changes that these verses call you to make. Your may want to write your discoveries in your spiritual journal.

As you study the additional Bible readings, try to make connections between them and the passage from 1 Timothy. In Jeremiah 32:1–3a, 6–15, God calls the prophet to buy land even though the prophet knows that the Babylonians will soon overtake the Judeans. He, however, responds in faith. In Psalm 91:1–6, 14–16, the writer meditates on God's protection of those who are faithful. Psalm 146 also praises God for helping those in need. Amos 6:1a, 4–7, warns that those Israelites who mistakenly put their confidence in luxurious possessions will be the first to be sent into exile. In Luke 16:19–31 Jesus tells the parable of the rich man who refuses to help one who is in need.

> *Helper of all who call upon your name, give me the wisdom to live as a faithful disciple of Jesus. Amen.*

Engage the Word

- What can readers of 1 Timothy learn about living faithfully?

Among second- and third-generation Christians of the first century, the practice of writing in the name of famous, deceased first-generation Christians was widespread. These later writers would speak in their predecessors' names in order to address new historical situations and problems with their authority.

Someone in the third Christian generation (toward the end of the first century or the beginning of the second) probably wrote 1 Timothy, 2 Timothy, and Titus in Paul's name to let him address that time and meet the needs of the church then. Differences in vocabulary, style, historical setting, and theological emphases (revealed by comparing them with Paul's known letters from the fifties) have led most scholars to this conclusion.

After his martyrdom in the fifties, early Christians used the apostle Paul's name to uphold traditions, clarify the present scene, and provide a personal example of one who has kept the faith. These three letters are called the Pastorals because of their pastoral concern for sound teaching, worship, organization, and ethical conduct. These writings sought to firm up the belief, structure, and life of the church.

Today's Bible reading is part of the First Letter to Timothy in which leaders are admonished to "teach and urge these duties"

(6:2). The negative traits of teachers who disagree with sound teaching are rehearsed in 6:3–5. The last negative trait listed is to imagine "that godliness [piety, religion] is a means of gain"—that religion ought to turn a profit (6:5).

These negative words lead into today's reading from 1 Timothy 6:6–19. According to 6:6, "there is great gain in godliness," but that great gain has nothing to do with material goods and riches. Rather, "the love of money is a root of all kinds of evil" (6:10). To put money first causes people to wander from the faith and finally be pierced with pain (6:10; 6:17–19 returns later to a concern for riches and their proper use).

From a leader's negative traits, the writer turns positive: "right-eousness, godliness, faith, love, endurance, gentleness," "the good fight of the faith" (6:11–12). In Paul's own letters, "faith" is the dynamic response to God's deed in Christ. Here, "the faith" has become doctrine/creedal formula (see 2:5, 3:16).

First Timothy 6:11–16 could have been part of an early Christian ordination service. The language seems very liturgical. These words that charge a person also confess God as Creator at the beginning ("who gives life to all"), as concluded at the end (at Jesus' final coming), as the blessed and only Sovereign God.

But the good faith is not first making wonderful confessions about God. It is entering into a relationship with God in Jesus Christ that takes hold of eternal life (6:12). It is in doing good, being rich in good works, generous, and ready to share, so as to "take hold of the life that really is life" (6:18–19). Entering into such life will make verbal confessions genuine.

Respond to the Word

- What can you and members of your church do to be more responsible and accountable as people of faith?
- What action will you take to be a more faithful disciple?

Go with the Word

Gentle God, hear our sins and have mercy on us.

> *Forgive us the words we have said which have given pain, and*
> *the words we have left unsaid which might have given hope.*
> *Forgive us the actions we have taken which have harmed*
> *friend or stranger, and the things undone which*
> *could have made a difference.*
> *Forgive us the thoughts which poison ourselves and*
> *deprecate others, and the thoughtlessness*
> *which ignores caring and worship.*

Gentle God, have mercy on us and give us peace. Amen.

Maren C. Tirabassi and Joan Jordan Grant, *An Improbable Gift of Blessing: Prayers and Affirmations to Nurture the Spirit* (Cleveland, Ohio: United Church Press, 1998), 139. Used by permission.

A G r a n d m o t h e r ' s F a i t h

I am reminded of your sincere faith, a faith that lived first in your grandmother Lois and your mother Eunice and now, I am sure, lives in you. For this reason I remind you to rekindle the gift of God that is within you through the laying on of my hands; for God did not give us a spirit of cowardice, but rather a spirit of power and of love and of self-discipline.

2 Timothy 1:5–7

Bible Reading: 2 Timothy 1:1–14

Additional Bible Readings: Lamentations 1:1–6/
Lamentations 3:19–26 (or Psalm 137)
or Habakkuk 1:1–4, 2:1–4/Psalm 37:1–9
Luke 17:5–10

Enter the Word

- How is faith passed from one generation to the next?
- Who are your own spiritual ancestors?

Reflect on the ways in which your faith has been passed on to you from previous generations. Perhaps you can name parents, grandparents, aunts and uncles, teachers, neighbors, and church members who influenced your faith journey. Moreover, prior generations are able to speak today through the Bible itself.

As you read 2 Timothy 1:1–14, note how faithful persons pave the way for Timothy and invite him to travel the road of Christian discipleship with them.

Also read the two passages from Lamentations in which the author cries over the despoiled Jerusalem and mourns because of his homelessness. Psalm 137 also laments the destruction of Jerusalem by Israel's enemies, the Babylonians. In Habakkuk, the prophet complains that God does not act while the faithless persecute God's people, but he soon indicates a large measure of confidence in God's willingness to reply. Psalm 37:1–9, a wisdom psalm, calls readers to trust in God and not be discouraged by the injustices around them. Luke 17:5–10 speaks both of faith and of obedience to God, which is to be understood as an obligation, not a reason for special reward.

> *Holy God, empower me with the love and self-discipline I need to live faithfully so that others might be drawn to you through my example and witness. Amen.*

Engage the Word

- How does 2 Timothy connect with an earlier generation of Christians and with our own generation as well?

Like last week's text from 1 Timothy, today's passage from 2 Timothy also most likely was written in Paul's name during the third Christian generation. In this personal letter, the writer lets Paul's voice speak to encourage church leaders to keep the faith.

In the form of a letter from Paul to his younger coworker Timothy, the writer wanted to help firm up these leaders' faith and teaching and call them to courageous testimony. After a typical greeting (2 Timothy: 1:1–2, though Paul's own letters used "grace and peace" instead of "grace, mercy, and peace"), the letter proceeds.

The earlier generations were indispensable bases for the present. For someone in a later generation to write in Paul's name would link the present generation to the past, thereby assuring that present faith rested on earlier firm foundations. (Note also 2 Timothy 2:1–2.)

But what is particularly striking is that, in a church that

silenced women (note 1 Timothy 2:8–15), the text lifted up two women as transmitters of a living faith. They could not have kept silent if they were to have an impact on the next generation.

However, for the writer, the lively faith of first and second generation Christians was in danger of waning; or at least there was the danger of burnout among church leaders. The writer calls for rekindling God's gift received at ordination (2 Timothy 1:6).

That gift did not demand cowardice but power, love, and self-discipline (1:7). It did not call for being ashamed of testifying but, relying on God's power, for being willing to suffer for the gospel (1:8; note Romans 1:16).

In keeping with the concern for sound teaching expressed in 1 and 2 Timothy and Titus (known as the Pastorals), 2 Timothy 1:9–10 takes on an almost creedal character to describe God's action: God saves; God calls on the basis of grace; that grace is eternal but now has appeared in the Savior Jesus Christ; the gospel of Jesus has done away with death and brought life and immortality to light. For the writer this understanding is part of sound teaching.

To lift Paul up as a great example, 2 Timothy 1:11–14 speaks of him as herald (preacher), apostle, and teacher (though in his own letters Paul never gives himself the title of preacher or teacher). Paul is one willing to suffer, unashamed to put his trust in God and hold fast to sound teaching. With the help of the Holy Spirit, those who stand in the tradition of Paul are to do the same.

To let Paul speak in the first person to Timothy makes for a personal and powerful way of communication. Now readers can put themselves in the person of Timothy and let Paul speak his word of faith and love and joy that spans generations.

Respond to the Word

- What is your congregation doing to pass its faith and traditions to the next generation? What else could you do?
- How can you be a mentor to a younger person in the Christian faith?

Go with the Word

Holy God, we remember, and we weep. We remember our mothers and fathers, our grandparents in the faith. We recall times when our faith was strong, when our churches were centers of community. Our tears flow with a sense of loss. We are not happy with what we have become: consumers of religion, not disciples of Jesus; captive to the latest fads, not innovators with a treasure to share.

We pray with the apostles, "Increase our faith!" But we are not daring enough to nourish the mustard seed. For faith, we know, is not an intellectual exercise but a matter of trust, and, God, we have forgotten how to trust. We have grave reservations about spiritual matters—about factors we cannot measure and a God we cannot see. So we pray without expectancy and we live without an eternal reference point. How can we sing the songs of faith in a secular society?

Amazing God, you come to us in spite of our laments, despite our cowardice, in the midst of our doubts. You rekindle your gifts within us. Thank you for a spirit of power and of love and of self-discipline. Thank you for abolishing death and granting us new life. Thank you for enlisting us as servants among your lost children, as teachers of your Word, as apostles of light. You have offered us the help of the Holy Spirit. You have promised us your grace to carry us beyond the limits of our own works. O God, as we accept our holy calling, we are filled with joy. Receive now our renewed commitment.

Amen.

Lavon and Bob Bayler, eds., *When We Pray: A Prayer Journal for Pastors and Worship Leaders,* Year C (Cleveland, Ohio: United Church Press, 1997), 103. Used by permission.

God's Awesome Deeds

All the earth worships you; they sing praises to you, sing praises to your name. Come and see what God has done; God does awesome deeds among mortals.

Psalm 66:4–5

Bible Reading: Psalm 66:1–12

Additional Bible Readings: Jeremiah 29:1, 4–7
                                 or 2 Kings 5:1–3, 7–15c/Psalm 111
                                 2 Timothy 2:8–15
                                 Luke 17:11–19

Enter the Word

- What amazing acts has God performed?
- When has one of God's deeds overwhelmed you with awe?

When we think about the greatness of God—the awe and wonder of our Creator, we are reminded of how small we are. The experience of awe is not limited to encounters with the natural creation. God's most awesome deeds are with people. The biblical stories of covenant, salvation, promise, and hope speak of God's awesome deeds among human beings. Although humans have strayed again and again, we continue to be loved and claimed by God. We can feel awed when we find ourselves called, redeemed, and made new as God's people.

Read Psalm 66:1–12. This psalmist recounts the ways God watched over the chosen people. References to the Exodus in this account and throughout the Hebrew Scriptures demonstrate that awe and worship of God comes from a recognition of being saved as well as from an appreciation for nature. Consider those times when God "turned the sea into dry land" for you, when you were kept "among the living," and when you were brought "to a spacious place."

Read the additional scriptures. Psalm 111 praises God for great deeds, especially for God's faithfulness to the covenant. Second Kings 5:1–3, 7–15c, tells the story of the prophet Elisha's healing of Naaman, who had leprosy. The story of Jesus' encounter with ten lepers is found in Luke 17:11–19. While nine went on their way, one of the healed persons recognized and responded to the awesome deed that had been performed. Jeremiah 29:1, 4–7, records a letter from the prophet to the exiles in Babylon that urges them to live normal lives because God is with them. Second Timothy 2:8–15 assures us of salvation in Christ whom God raised from the dead.

I sing praise for your awesome deeds, O God. Amen.

Engage the Word

- What reasons does the psalmist have for praising God?

Psalms is Israel's prayer and song book. The psalms represent a collection of hymns and prayers that arose out of the life of Israel over many generations. They reflect the full range of human experience and responses to God, from the depths of anguish and despair to the heights of thanksgiving and praise. Today's psalm represents the latter: praise of God's awesome deeds.

Psalms often are a mixture of words addressed to the people (telling them something or calling them to do something) and words addressed to God in prayer. In Psalm 66, verses 1–3 are a call to the people; verse 4 is a prayer to God. Verses 5–9 are words to the people; verses 10–12 are words to God. There is a rhythm between speaking to the people and speaking to God. Prayer to God and proclamation to the people belong together.

As the psalmist begins Psalm 66 with a call for "joyful noise to God," it is not simply a call to Israel. It is a call to "all the earth." Some psalms speak not only in terms of people but of all nature (note Psalm 148:7–10). God is not only Israel's God. God is the awesome Creator of all things and all peoples. God has power over those who oppose God's good purposes (Psalm 66:3) and deserves worship and praise. To sing glory to God's name is to sing glory to God's being and to all for which God stands.

But having begun Psalm 66 by addressing "all the earth" and offering a prayer to God (66:4), the psalmist becomes specific and refers to Israel's experience. Israel knew God's liberating power in their deliverance from Egypt. The words of verse 6, "turned the sea into dry land," clearly refer to the Exodus and to Israel's rejoicing over what God had done for them.

Yet the psalmist does not linger long simply on Israel's experience. Verse 7 turns again to "the nations" and God's watch over them. God wants no rebellion on the part either of Israel or other nations of the world. For a nation to put itself first is to commit idolatry. All peoples are to praise God (66:8).

God is the One who has kept Israel alive and guided the people in a good path (66:9). Yet, in prayer, the psalmist confesses that God has tested their loyalty and the purity of their commitment (66:10). God has not saved them from tough times as they wandered from Egypt through the wilderness (66:11–12), but God did bring them finally to a "spacious place," free from oppression in the Promised Land.

In the reading from Jeremiah, the prophet points to the tough experience of exile in a foreign land, but he calls for a positive response in terms of building and planting, marrying and having children, and seeking the welfare of the city to make it (in the words of the psalm) a "spacious place."

The Second Letter to Timothy speaks of suffering hardship for standing up for the gospel, but this hardship leads to "salvation . . . with eternal glory" (2 Timothy 2:10) and dying with Christ leads to life with him. In Luke, Jesus healed a man with leprosy who gave thanks and praised God. God's awesome deeds deserve a "joyful noise."

Respond to the Word

- How can you, like the psalmist, help people to recognize and sing praise for God's awesome deeds?
- What words of praise will you offer to God this week?

Go with the Word

Thanksgiving psalms speak of the personal experience of a new order. . . . Surprises and newness overcome the old way of looking at the world. . . . Thanksgivings tell the story of the past distress and of God's saving reversal of the situation. . . . [They] give testimony for conversion. In telling our story of wonder and awe, we are evangelists, calling people to a life of faith in this God who has saved us.

Denise Dombkowski Hopkins, *Journey Through the Psalms: A Path to Wholeness* (New York: United Church Press, 1990). Used by permission.

Words, Sweeter than Honey

How sweet are your words to my taste, sweeter than honey to my mouth! Through your precepts I get understanding; therefore I hate every false way.

Psalm 119:103–104

Bible Reading: Psalm 119:97–104

Additional Bible Readings: Jeremiah 31:27–34
or Genesis 32:22–31/Psalm 121
2 Timothy 3:14–4:5
Luke 18:1–8

Enter the Word

- Why might the psalmist describe God's words as "sweeter than honey"?
- How would you describe the taste of God's words?

The psalmist writes about loving the law of God and compares the words of the law to the sweetness of honey. As you read Psalm 119:97–104 think about the first time you tasted honey. Perhaps a parent or grandparent helped you spread honey on a biscuit. Recall the pleasant taste of sweet food in your mouth.

Now think for a moment about words that have been spoken to you—words that were as sweet as honey. Remember the one who spoke those words to you and why you cherished the words.

God too has spoken to us with sweet words that come from the deepest love in the universe. God's law gives us wisdom and understanding, freedom and joy. The words of love and justice have become the sweet words of God's respect for our ability to respond to humanity. We are asked to love God because God first loved us.

The psalmist who wrote that God's words are sweeter than honey knew that the words asked for obedience—and the psalmist rejoiced and turned from all evil ways. The Word of God is filled with directives, but each command comes from God's unflagging love of all humanity and from God's wish that we return our love to God by loving one another without question.

Read the other passages for today and link them to Psalm 119.

> *Let me taste and see that your words, O God, add sweet-*
> *ness and joy to my life. Amen.*

Engage the Word

* How does the psalmist's attitude toward God's Torah affect the way he lives?

Like last Sunday, the word for today is from Psalms. Psalm 119 is the longest psalm and praises God's Torah, God's teaching of a way of life that responds to God's liberating grace in the Exodus from Egypt. The Hebrew word *Torah* is often translated as "law," but it is more than a series of laws. It is a way of life that is God's gift, to which one responds in gratitude. It is an injustice to think of "law" as rules to evoke God's grace. To keep the law is to respond to the grace God already has shown.

Sometimes *Torah* is used to describe the first five books of the Bible. These books are the part of the Hebrew Scriptures that became Israel's first official writings, their canon ("measuring stick" or "norm"). For the psalmist, these writings witness to God's teaching of a way of life.

Psalm 119 has a remarkable structure. It is a carefully crafted alphabetic poem that works through the twenty-two letters of the Hebrew alphabet. Each stanza has eight lines, all beginning with the same letter, so 22 (letters) x 8 (lines) = 176 verses. With such poetic devotion, the psalmist expresses full praise for God's gift. As the reader moves through verses 97–104, it is possible to note a number of words that become synonyms for Torah or "law": commandment, decrees, precepts, word, ordinances.

For the psalmist, God's law is not some heavy burden. It is something to love and meditate on continuously (Psalm 119:97). It is always with the psalmist to give wisdom to counter enemies (119:98). To meditate on the law gives one more understanding than that imparted by official teachers or by the aged (119:99–100). Thus God's gift of this teaching surpasses even the best that any human being can communicate.

Sometimes God's law is understood as a fence to keep a person within good ways. As a fence, it holds an individual back from walking in evil ways (119:101). It is a teaching from which one is never to turn away (119:102). It is a protection from going in false ways. In verse 97, the psalmist states his love for God's way and then in verse 104 proclaims to "hate every false way."

God's word and way do not leave a bad taste in the psalmist's mouth. They are "sweeter than honey" (119:103). In contrast, Jeremiah states: "The parents have eaten sour grapes, and the children's teeth are set on edge" (Jeremiah 31:29). In Jeremiah 31:33–34, the prophet comments that God's gift of forgiveness is to lead to the sweetness of a new covenant relationship with God.

Just as Psalm 119 reflects on God's Torah in Israel's scriptures, so does the statement in 2 Timothy 3:15–16 that refers to "sacred writings" as "useful for teaching, for reproof, for correction, and for training in righteousness."

In another reading for today, Luke 18:1, Jesus lifts up the "need to pray always and not to lose heart." That concept is in harmony with the thoughts of the psalmist, who meditates "all the day long" (119:97) on God's will and way, which is so worthy of celebration and praise.

Respond to the Word

- How might you and a group you study with practice the psalmist's devotion to God's word on a daily basis?
- In what ways will you celebrate God's word, given to you through the Scriptures?

Go with the Word

I read the Torah as Jews have read it and loved it for centuries. For example, I can tell you what is the middle word in the Torah. I can tell you what is the middle letter in the Torah. Over the generations Jewish scholars have read the Torah not as a novel to see how it ends, but as a love letter. For instance, "Why did he use this word instead of that word?" "Why is there a space here?" "Why a comma here instead of a period?" That's the way you read a love letter and wonder, "What did he or she mean by this word?" We Jews have seen the Torah as not just a book of stories or law codes, but as a love letter from God.

Harold Kushner, *Questions of Faith: Contemporary Thinkers Respond,*
ed. Dolly Patterson (Philadelphia: Trinity Press International, 1990), 64.

God's Spirit Poured Out

Then afterward I will pour out my spirit on all flesh; your sons and daughters shall prophesy, your old men shall dream dreams, and your young men shall see visions. Even on the male and female slaves, in those days, I will pour out my spirit.

Joel 2:28–29

Bible Reading: Joel 2:23–32

Additional Bible Readings: Psalm 65
                                           or Jeremiah 14:7–10, 19–22/
                                              Psalm 84:1–7
                                           2 Timothy 4:6–8, 16–18
                                           Luke 18:9–14

Enter the Word

- What might be some signs of the presence of God's Spirit?
- How has God's Spirit been poured out in your own life?

Read Joel 2:23–32. These words may prompt you to remember a dream or vision that gave you guidance from God or had an impact on you in some other way.

Joel states that the Spirit of God will cause the old to dream and the young to have visions and to prophesy (Joel 2:28). Think about the implications of these words for your own life. Ponder ways that an infilling of God's Spirit has changed—or could change—you.

Also consider the impact of the gift of the Spirit on people who are open to receive this blessing. Close your eyes and try to envision the world transformed by God's Spirit. Imagine the end of poverty and famine, the peace of resolved conflicts. Try to picture the faces of those you know who seem filled with the Spirit. Then picture yourself glowing with the Spirit.

Continue your study by reading the additional passages for today and relating them to Joel's prophecy.

> *Let your Spirit so fill me and the whole earth, Holy God, that all people may experience and celebrate your presence. Amen.*

Engage the Word

- How might Joel's words have influenced those who heard it?

In Israel's long history, prophets spoke for God and sought to speak God's truth for their times. They were not primarily predictors of the future but voices for God's truth in the present, though that truth did have future implications for the life of Israel.

Some of those prophets were outside the official religious establishment and challenged both political and religious leaders for their unfaithfulness. Others stood within the official religious establishment and spoke their words in that context. Joel appears to have been that kind of prophet, related to the worship in the Temple, about four hundred years before Jesus came.

This means that he did his work after the Exile in Babylon and at the time of rebuilding the life of the people in their homeland in Palestine. Joel was part of the worship and cultic life of the people, calling them to prayer and fasting, telling the priests to gather the people, giving instructions for prayer, and proclaiming God's response to the people's honest prayers.

The book of Joel is divided into two parts. In Joel 1:2–2:17, the prophet calls for a service of complaint and petition to God. In Joel 2:18–3:21, the mood is very different. The people have repented, and God promises salvation and assures them that their prayers have been heard. Today's Bible reading from Joel 2:23–32 is part of that second section.

After giving assurance of food to the animals (Joel 2:21–22),

Joel calls the people of Israel to be glad and rejoice over God's gift of material prosperity. Now there is plenty of rain and plenty of grain and wine (2:22–24) after the lean years of devouring locusts caused by the people's unfaithfulness to God (2:25).

Now they will have plenty to eat. They are to sing praises for God's wonderful dealing with them, and God promises that they never again are to be put to shame (2:26). Because of this material prosperity, they are to know that God is with them as the one and only God (2:27). Material prosperity is a reason to be glad and to rejoice in God.

Joel then moves beyond material prosperity to proclaim something more. He announces the outpouring of God's Spirit (a text that Luke quotes in the Pentecost story in Acts 2:17–21). Deeper than external material prosperity is the internal spiritual power that enables both men and women to prophesy ("speak for" God), to dream dreams and see visions (Joel 2:28–29, dreams and visions that portend the day of judgment, as verses 30–32 show). What is important is that God pours out the Spirit on *all* flesh, all people, male and female, empowering them to be instruments of God's prophetic and imaginative word.

The additional readings for today support the concepts presented in Joel. Psalm 65 also praises God for water and earth's bounty (65:9–11), as well as for the nearness of God to all (65:1–4). In 2 Timothy, God stands by and gives strength for proclaiming the message (4:17). In Luke 18:9–14, Jesus' parable points to the true way to know and receive God's restoring mercy. God wants all people to know the gift of God's empowering Spirit.

Respond to the Word

- How can you and your congregation show forth God's Spirit in specific ways this week?
- What changes will you make in your dealings with others as you recognize that God's Spirit is available to *all* people?

Go with the Word

The Holy Spirit is life that gives life,
Moving all things.
It is the root in every creature
And purifies all things,
Wiping away our sins, anointing our wounds.
It is radiant life, worthy of praise,
Awakening and enlivening all things.

Hildegard of Bingen, "Antiphon for the Holy Spirit I," in *Hildegard of Bingen: Mystical Writings*, ed. Fiona Bowie and Oliver Davies, trans. Robert Carver (New York: Crossroad, 1990), 118. Used by permission of Crossroad and SPCK.

Z a c c h a e u s ,   C o m e   D o w n !

When Jesus came to the place, he looked and said to Zacchaeus, "Zacchaeus, hurry and come down; for I must stay at your house today." So Zacchaeus hurried down and was happy to welcome Jesus. All who saw it began to grumble and said, "He has gone to be the guest of one who is a sinner." Zacchaeus stood there and said to Jesus, "Look, half of my possessions I will give to the poor; and if I have defrauded anyone of anything, I will pay back four times as much."

Luke 19:5–8

Bible Reading:	Luke 19:1–10
Additional Bible Readings:	Habakkuk 1:1–4, 2:1–4/ Psalm 119:137–144 or Isaiah 1:10–18/Psalm 32:1–7 2 Thessalonians 1:1–4, 11–12

Enter the Word

- Why might Jesus have called Zacchaeus to be his host?
- When has your view of Jesus been so obstructed that you figuratively had to climb a tree to see him?

38

As you study Luke 19:1–10, note the points of identity or kinship that you feel. In many ways, Zacchaeus represents us all.

After you read the passage about Zacchaeus, set aside time for this self-guided meditation.

> *See yourself looking up at a tall sycamore tree. Feel the breeze, the bending branches, and the soft leaves as you climb the tree. Experience your emotions as you sit nestled in a branch. Imagine that you see Jesus. Jesus calls your name and invites you to come down from the tree. Climb down now from the tree. Picture yourself and esus doing something specific together. See yourself as you respond to God's love.*

Read the text from Luke again. Ponder what Zacchaeus had heard about Jesus that moved him to climb the sycamore for an unobstructed view. Consider what Zacchaeus might have expected Jesus to do for him. Contemplate ways you are like Zacchaeus.

As you read the additional passages from Habakkuk, Isaiah, 2 Thessalonians, and the Psalms, relate them to Luke's story.

> *Compassionate God, help me to overcome any obstacles that prevent me from being near you and doing your will. Amen.*

Engage the Word

- Why might the story of Zacchaeus have been especially meaningful to Luke's audience?

Writing toward the end of the first century, Luke had strong desires to break through human barriers of nation and language, gender and race, religion and social class. For Luke, Jesus meant "good news of great joy for all the people" (Luke 2:10), and Acts is the story of apostles and Paul taking that good news across the Roman Empire.

The Gospel of Luke tells the story of outreach to those whom the religious establishment of Jesus' day often rejected: to outcast shepherds and despised Samaritans, to a dying criminal and some murderous Roman soldiers, to subjugated women and persons shunned because of their disabilities.

In Luke 19:1–10, Jesus reached out to a rejected tax collector. Zacchaeus was despised by his own Jewish people as a sinner who collaborated with the hated Romans in collecting taxes for them. He was free to add on to that tax for his individual benefit at the expense of his own people; and he got rich doing so.

In spite of (or is it because of?) his wealth, Zacchaeus apparently was not a happy man; and when he heard that Jesus was coming, this small-of-stature man climbed a tree to see him. What a surprise when Jesus looked up at him and called his name, Zacchaeus. The name means "righteous one," but with his ill-gotten gain, Zacchaeus' life had been anything but righteous.

Yet Jesus' call to this tax collector and his going home with him was not the end—it was the beginning of a whole new life for Zacchaeus. He not only had a personal relationship with Jesus and the presence of Jesus in his home but his encounter with Jesus also made Zacchaeus an honest man. No longer would he defraud people, and any whom he had defrauded would be repaid fourfold (twice the amount the law demanded). His encounter also gave him a whole new sense of responsibility for the poor. He gave half of what he possessed to them.

After all this Jesus said to Zacchaeus, "Today salvation [God's health] has come to this house" (Luke 19:9). Now he could be a true child of Abraham as one who could share the promise to Abraham to be a blessing. Now he had experienced what it was to move from being lost to being found and transformed by Jesus.

Now Zacchaeus could live out his name, "righteous one," and exemplify the words, *the righteous live by their faith* (Habakkuk 2:4). Zacchaeus could also respond to the righteous God of Psalm 119. Now he could be the kind of person of faith and love for whom the writer of 2 Thessalonians would give thanks (1:3).

When Jesus breaks through barriers and transforms life, God is at work to bring "good news of great joy for all people" (Luke 2:10).

Respond to the Word

- Zacchaeus' story suggests how God can transform persons whom religious folks might label "sinners." How can you help others to recognize this transforming power?
- What amends will you make to people you have somehow cheated or harmed?

Go with the Word

Up Where You Can See

All: Sometimes you just gotta get up where you can see.

One: A short man climbed a tree.

All: Sometimes you just gotta get up where you can see.

One: Jesus called him down and entered his life.

All: Sometimes you just gotta get up where you can see.

One: It usually isn't that simple. Most people don't see things clearly the first time.

All: Sometimes you just gotta get up where you can see.

One: There are barriers which prevent real changes.

All: Sometimes you just gotta get up where you can see.

One: Dear God, open our eyes.

All: Sometimes you just gotta get up where you can see.

One: Dear God, open our minds.

All: Sometimes you just gotta get up where you can see.

One: Dear God, open our hearts.

All: Sometimes you just gotta get up where you can see.

One: Help us get up where we can see you more clearly.

All: Sometimes you just gotta get up where you can see.

The Inviting Word, Older Youth Learner's Guide (Cleveland: United
Church Press, 1995), 25. Used by permission.

E t e r n a l   C o m f o r t ,   G o o d   H o p e

Now may our Lord Jesus Christ himself and God our

Parent, who loved us and through grace gave us eternal

comfort and good hope, comfort your hearts and

strengthen them in every good work and word.

2 Thessalonians 2:16–17

Bible Reading: 2 Thessalonians 2:1–5, 13–17

Additional Bible Readings: Haggai 1:15b–2:9/
      Psalm 145:1–5, 17–21 (or Psalm 98)
    or Job 19:23–27a/Psalm 17:1–9
    Luke 20:27–38

Enter the Word

- How might God's comfort and hope encourage and empower us?
- What comfort and hope do you need from God right now?

Before you read 2 Thessalonians, take a look at the painting *Caged Bird* on the last page of this lesson. Reflect on times in which you have felt like a bird in a cage. Perhaps in some ways you feel that way now. Identify the fears or problems that make you feel like that. Think about how the door of the cage could be opened, enabling you to free yourself from the fears and problems that confine you.

Read 2 Thessalonians 2:1–5 and 13–17, a passage that calls us to explore God's hope and comfort. Read verses 13–17 again but this time replace the word "you" with your own name. This message is for you! You are a gift to your church. Consider the ways that you use your talents in God's service. The Spirit has called you through the gospel so that you may have the glory of Jesus Christ. Rejoice that God's grace is with you, as is God's comfort and hope, to sustain you in every good work and word.

In the additional readings, Job 19:23–27a affirms that his Redeemer lives. Jesus proclaims that God is the God of the living in Luke 20:27–38. In Psalm 17:1–9, the psalmist cries out for deliverance from his enemies. The writer of Psalm 98 calls people to worship God who will establish a sovereign rule on earth, while Psalm 145:1–5, 17–21 proclaims God's greatness and goodness. The prophet Haggai calls the people to rebuild God's temple.

> *God, comfort and give me hope that I may be free even in situations that confine me. Amen.*

Engage the Word

- How might this letter have encouraged the Thessalonians to continue living and working as they awaited the return of Christ?

The Second Letter to the Thessalonians is one of several New Testament writings, written in the name of the Apostle Paul, but whose authors actually may have written after Paul's death. They let "Paul" speak in later settings to new issues. The other letters that fall into this category are Colossians, Ephesians, 1 and 2 Timothy, and Titus. This practice of writing in someone else's name was widespread in both Jewish and Christian circles. This custom allowed authoritative persons from the past to "speak" to the present when they were no longer alive to speak for themselves.

A careful examination of vocabularies, writing styles, potential historical contexts, and theological emphases cause scholars to raise questions of authorship. Significant differences along these lines between First Thessalonians and Second Thessalonians raise questions about Paul's authorship. (Note how strongly the writer wants to present Paul as the writer in 2 Thessalonians 3:17).

The way 2 Thessalonians speaks about the final coming of Jesus differs both from 1 Thessalonians and Paul's other known letters. Its apocalyptic (revelational) images of the end (see also 2:6–12) are more akin to the Revelation of John and texts like Mark 13, which were both written after Paul's death in different settings than Paul's letters.

Paul's own letters, including 1 Thessalonians, expected Jesus to come again soon. Second Thessalonians 2:1–3 seems to challenge that expectation and met the problem of a delayed coming by affirming no premature expectation. The references to "rebellion" and "the lawless one" who "exalts himself above every so-called god or object of worship, so that he takes his seat in the temple of God, declaring himself to be God" (2:3–4), suggest the emperor worship that Christians were persecuted for resisting.

Given that context, part of 2 Thessalonians strongly affirms the faith of the Thessalonians (2:13–14) and calls them to "stand firm and hold fast to the traditions" of Paul (2:15). Then follows a "benediction" (good word) for them. It calls for Jesus and God to comfort their hearts and strengthen them for every good work and word, a call based on God's love and the grace of God's gift of comfort and hope.

The noun and the verb "comfort" translate a Greek word that means literally "called alongside." Jesus and God are "alongside" us to give strength. The word "comfort" with its Latin roots means literally "with strength." Comfort is more than a pat on the back. It is Jesus and God's presence to strengthen us in the present and give us good hope for an eternal future.

The Haggai reading from after the Exile proclaims God's presence with them (Haggai 2:4–5) as they rebuild a splendid Temple. Psalm 145 praises God's mighty acts and glorious splendor and proclaims God's justice, kindness, and nearness (145:4–5, 17–18). In Luke 20:38, Jesus proclaims the resurrecting God of the living. God's presence with us empowers us with courage, comfort, and hope.

Respond to the Word

- How can you and others bring God's comfort to those who are fearful or beset by problems?
- What situations will you turn over to God in order to find comfort and hope in your own life?

Go with the Word

Walter Williams, *Caged Bird*, The Amistad Research Center, New
Orleans, Louisiana. Used by permission.

By Your Endurance

They asked Jesus, "Teacher, when will this be?" And Jesus said, "Beware that you are not led astray; for many will come in my name and say 'I am the one!' and, 'The time is near!' Do not go after them. You will be hated by all because of my name. But not a hair of your head will perish. By your endurance you will gain your lives."

Luke 21:7a, 8, 17–19

Bible Reading: Luke 21:5–19

Additional Bible Readings: Isaiah 65:17–25/Isaiah 12
or Malachi 4:1–2a/Psalm 98
2 Thessalonians 3:6–13

Enter the Word

- What resources or traits help persons to endure tough times?
- What burdensome situations have you endured and survived?

In Luke 21:5–19 Jesus speaks about the destruction of the Temple as a sign that the end is nearing. Other signs of the end will follow, but before they do the disciples of Christ will be persecuted, betrayed, and hated. Through endurance, these disciples will gain their souls. After you read this passage, imagine things in the lives of these first-century disciples that demanded endurance. Then consider the situations in your own life that require endurance.

God will provide resources for faithful people to endure tough times of illness, unemployment, separation, the death of a loved one, poverty, homelessness, and other difficult circumstances. In your spiritual journal make a list of resources you are aware of that can enable you to survive hard times. Give thanks for all of the physical, emotional, social, intellectual, and spiritual resources at your disposal.

As you explore the additional Bible readings for this week, look for connections between them and the passage from Luke 21.

> *Faithful God, empower me in times of trouble and stress*
> *so that I may know you are with me. Amen.*

Engage the Word

- How does Luke's interpretation of Jesus' words strengthen his own community of faith so that they might endure?

Interpreters of the Gospels must remember that the texts interweave material from three time frames: the time of Jesus, the time between Jesus and the writing of the Gospels, and the time of the Gospel writers themselves. We have direct access only to the third time frame because we have the Gospels. They reflect material that spanned a forty-year oral process of teaching and preaching among early Christians before there were any written Gospels, and that material reflects traditions that go back to Jesus' life and ministry.

The Gospel writers creatively shaped and reshaped these materials to meet the needs of their own particular communities. Consequently, these various time frames interact with one another. For instance, the way Luke tells the story of Jesus in his time will be affected by Luke's situation in his own era. Thus, Luke's telling the story of Jesus is not a "facts and figures" history but an *interpreted* history to speak to Luke's time.

Luke wrote toward the end of the first century after the destruction of Jerusalem in 70 C.E. This knowledge (Luke 21:24) affected the way in which he recounts Jesus' word about the destruction of the Temple in Jerusalem (21:5–6). For Jesus, that event was still in the future. For Luke, it was in the past.

With their expectation that history would end soon, first-generation Christians joined Jerusalem's destruction with Jesus' coming and the world's end. But Luke wrote well into the second or even third generation. He knew that the end had not come. He separated Jerusalem's destruction from the end of history and prepared his readers for the longer haul. They were not to be misled by those who say, "The time is near!" (21:8).

Wars, insurrections, and natural calamities happen, and Luke knew that; but these occurrences do not necessarily mean that the end is near (21:9–11). Followers of Jesus in his time and in the time after him, including the time of Luke's readers, can expect arrest and persecution from religious and political authorities for their commitment to Jesus (note Acts 4:1–4).

This continuing history was a time for testimony (Luke 21:13). God would give Jesus' followers the words and wisdom they needed to defend themselves and withstand opponents (21:14). They would know betrayal by family, death, and hatred (21:16–17). Yet, Jesus promised that by their endurance they would survive (21:18–19). *Psyche* in verse 19 is better translated by the word "life" than "soul," as it is in the New English Bible which reads: "By standing firm you will win true life for yourselves."

In contrast to Luke's portrayal of destruction, Isaiah 65 points to God's creating a new Jerusalem of joy and delight with no hurt or destruction; and Isaiah 12 speaks of joy in drawing water from the wells of salvation. Second Thessalonians says, "do not be weary in doing what is right" (3:13).

Times can be tough when standing firm for Jesus, but God is tougher and will be there beside us, not to hurt but to help.

Respond to the Word

- How can you be a resource for someone enduring tough times?
- What steps will you take to strengthen your relationship with God so as to be better prepared to endure difficult situations?

Go with the Word

The end is not yet. During the time of testimony, disciples will experience suffering. They are not exempt. There is nothing here of . . . an arrogance born of a doctrine of a rapture in which believers are removed from the scenes of persecution and suffering. There are no scenes here of cars crashing into one another on the highways because their drivers have been blissfully raptured. The word of Jesus in our lesson is still forceful: "This will give you an opportunity to testify . . . . By your endurance you will gain your souls."

Fred B. Craddock et. al., *Preaching Through the Christian Year: Year C*
(Valley Forge, Pa.: Trinity Press International, 1994), 474.

God Remembers

The child's father Zechariah was filled with the Holy Spirit and spoke this prophecy: "Blessed be the God of Israel, for God has looked favorably on God's people and redeemed them. God has shown the mercy promised to our ancestors, and has remembered God's holy covenant."

Luke 1:67–68, 72

Bible Reading: Luke 1:68–79

Additional Bible Readings: Jeremiah 23:1–6
or Jeremiah 23:1-6/Psalm 46
Colossians 1:11–20
Luke 23:33–43

Enter the Word

- In what ways does God remember people today?
- How do you know that God has remembered you?

Read Luke 1:68–79, the song of an old, childless man who had long since given up hope of being a father. He has just found out that he and his aging wife, Elizabeth, are to be parents of a special child. What joyous news.

Zechariah sings that God has remembered the covenant made with Israel—the covenant of the Messiah, the Savior. He sings that his child will come into this world to proclaim the Messiah. He is honored and grateful that God has chosen Elizabeth and him to be the parents of the prophet of the Most High.

God remembers God's people. Through all times the covenant has been at our reach, in our hands, and we celebrate it. We celebrate the Reign of Christ that was, that is, and that is to come.

The church year culminates and ends this week. On the Reign of Christ Sunday we celebrate the life, death, and resurrection of Jesus Christ, the Promised One. Next Sunday is the first Sunday of Advent, which begins the first season of the new church year.

Think about the year that has just passed. Recall important events, celebrations, and changes in your own life. Ponder the ways in which Christ was present in your life and faithful to you.

As you read the additional Bible passages, search for ways to relate them to Zechariah's song in Luke.

> *Remember me, O God, for my life depends upon the covenantal relationship I have with you through Jesus Christ. Amen.*

Engage the Word

- How does Zechariah's song help Luke's audience to understand John the Baptist's role in relation to Jesus?

Today's "psalm" is not from the Book of Psalms; it is the song of Zechariah (John the Baptist's father) as recorded in Luke 1:68–79. It rings with references to what the God of Israel has done in the past. The God at work in John the Baptist and Jesus is the same God at work in Abraham and David. Both John and Jesus were Jews. Their lives and ministries fulfilled their own heritage.

As Luke shaped the infancy stories (Luke 1–2), he wanted to emphasize the continuity between what God had done in Israel's history and what God had done in Jesus. For God to act with mercy in Jesus was to remember, that is, "to make present," God's covenant of mercy with Israel.

Zechariah's song has two parts. The first (Luke 1:68–75) focuses on Jesus as God's mighty Savior; the second (1:76–79) on John as God's preparing prophet. This structure is not incidental. Even before John is born, Luke shows him as subordinate to Jesus (note Luke 1:41–44). The Gospel writer wants to make the Messiah's identity clear (note Luke 3:15–16), for in Luke's time toward the end of the first century some people still saw John as the Messiah.

God had redeemed Israel from Egyptian bondage in the past. Now God was raising up a savior from David's line (1:69). The prophets spoke of salvation from enemies and hate (1:70–71). God was making present in Jesus the mercy promised in holy covenant to earlier ancestors and the oath of rescue sworn to Abraham, so that people might serve God without fear to make life holy and right all their days (1:72–75).

The previous verses of Zechariah's song are all third-person proclamations in blessing God. In verse 76 the song shifts to the second person with Zechariah addressing his own child as "the prophet of the Most High." As prophet, he is to "speak for" God and prepare the way for Jesus the Savior.

The verses that follow sing with some of the great words of the Hebrew Scriptures to describe the purpose of John's ministry: knowledge of salvation (God's health), forgiveness of sins, God's tender mercy, the dawn from on high, light in shadow of death, and the way of peace.

Luke has given us a moving picture of Zechariah singing this to the miracle child of his and Elizabeth's old age. Zechariah himself had known God's mercy, and now his son would be a prophet of God's mercy in Jesus.

Jeremiah pictures God as a gathering shepherd, and the prophet looks forward to an heir of David who will bring wisdom and justice, righteousness and safety (Jeremiah 23:3, 5–6). In Colossians 1:15–19, a Christ-hymn presents one of the most exalted pictures of Jesus, but it is the blood of the cross (the outpouring of God's love) that makes peace. Luke's depiction of Jesus' crucifixion tells of his ministry of forgiveness, even to his executioners, and his promise of paradise to the criminal beside him (Luke 23:33–43).

God remembers the covenant through the Reign of Christ from before his birth, through his death and resurrection.

Respond to the Word

- What can you do to help someone recognize God's faithfulness?
- What action will Zechariah's words prompt you to take today?

Go with the Word

Prayer of Confession

> *Almighty God,*
> *I come to you*
> *because I am struggling inside.*
> *I dwell on past hurts and heartaches*
> *and refuse to let them go and forgive.*
> *For that, forgive me.*
> *I spend so much time as a worrier,*
> *looking within,*
> *that I forget the promise of your [Child],*
> *given for me.*
> *For that I need forgiveness.*
> *I focus too many times on useless speculation of the*
> *unknown*
> *and fail to recall your promise*
> *of the Holy Spirit.*
> *Forgive me!*
> *For not remembering that you . . .*
> *live within and beside me*
> *Forever.*
> *Amen.*

"Prayer of Confession," from the Sunday service of worship,
International Fellowship of Metropolitan Community Church, Key
West, Florida. Used by permission.

WHAT you
goNNa Name
THAT pretty
Little Baby?

Oh, Mary, what you gonna
name that pretty
little Baby? Glory, Glory
to the new born King!
Some will call Him one
thing, but I think I'll
call Him Jesus! Glory,
Glory, Glory, Glory
to the new born King!

Aminah Brenda Lynn Robinson, *What You Gonna Name That Pretty
Little Baby?* in *The Teachings Drawn from African-American Spirituals*
(Orlando: Harcourt Brace & Co., 1992). Copyright © 1992 by
Aminah Brenda Lynn Robinson. Used by permission of Harcourt
Brace & Company.

Advent

During the four weeks preceding Christmas, the world eagerly anticipates the arrival of Emmanuel, God-with-us. The deep blue or purple used during this liturgical season points to the coming of royalty. Although this ruler of peace is unparalleled in all of human history, he did not arrive with pomp and regal splendor but was born in an animal shed and laid to sleep in a feeding trough.

The season of Advent heightens human awareness of God's reign. That reign breaks in upon us with the birth of Jesus, but it will be fully realized when Christ returns to judge and renew the earth. Advent, therefore, helps humanity to look back to Jesus' birth 2000 years ago and ahead to Christ's second coming.

Try to put yourself in Mary's place as she anticipates the birth of a child conceived by the power of the Holy Spirit. Then read Matthew 1:21–23. Imagine yourself as Joseph hearing those startling words from God's angel.

Look at the picture entitled *What You Gonna Name That Pretty Little Baby?* Think about what the name of Jesus means to you. Ponder how this child has changed human history in general and you in particular. Offer a prayer of thanks as you continue to await the celebration of his arrival.

Live in Expectation

Keep awake therefore, for you do not know on what day your Lord is coming. But understand this: if the owner of the house had known in what part of the night the thief was coming, the owner would have stayed awake and would not have let the house be broken into. Therefore you also must be ready, for God's future Ruler and Judge is coming at an unexpected hour.

Matthew 24:42–44

Bible Reading: Matthew 24:36–44

Additional Bible Readings:
Isaiah 2:1–5
Psalm 122
Romans 13:11–14

Enter the Word

- What expectations do many people have as Christmas approaches?
- How do you live in anticipation of Jesus' coming?

This week marks the beginning of Advent, a season of possibilities, a time of expectation. Begin your preparation by making a list of specific expectations that you have for this season of waiting and for the Christmas season that follows.

Now read Matthew 24:36–44, noting the images painted in words. You may want to sketch some of these images. Next, read

Romans 13:11–14, where Paul states that we know what time it is.

The promise of Advent, which looks to a time of hope and peace and justice, was envisioned by prophets before Jesus' birth. Read Isaiah 2:1–5 and Psalm 122. Living in expectation means making real changes in your life and in the world.

> *Gracious God, as I begin this season of waiting, empower me to be ever vigilant as I prepare for your coming. Amen.*

Engage the Word

- How would Matthew's urgent reminders to his community to "keep awake" have helped them be faithful, prepared followers of Christ?

"Keep awake!" "Be ready!" Matthew speaks with urgency as he reminds his community to prepare for the coming of Christ. Why did they need to remember to remain alert, to "live in expectation"?

Matthew wrote his Gospel after the fall of Jerusalem (70 C.E.) to a community with strong Jewish roots. Eager to present Jesus as the long-expected Messiah to the Jews, Matthew showed that Jesus represented not a contradiction to Judaism, but God's long-anticipated climax and completion of Judaic faith (Matthew 1:1–2:23; 5:17 20). Jesus was the promised ruler of whom the prophets spoke, whose ancestry can be traced back to King David and Abraham (1:1–17). He was the ruler of the Jews (27:11–31). Matthew challenged his readers to a higher level of obedience. Jesus Christ was the source of a higher righteousness, exceeding that of the scribes and Pharisees, that resulted in a new obedience to God. This obedience included the active and visible love of God and love of others (5:21–6:34; 23:1–39).

The concern for Jewish Christians in Matthew's Gospel extended to Gentiles as well. Matthew's post-Easter community included converts, both women and men, from all nations (28:16–20). God had always intended that Gentiles become a part of the church universal (4:12–5:1; 22:8–10).

Mark's Gospel was written a decade or so earlier than Matthew's, and Matthew faced a pastoral problem that had not been so acute at the time of Mark: the delay of Christ's final coming. As years passed and Jesus' coming *parousia* did not occur as many expected, some Christians in Matthew's community grew weary of waiting. Others were engaged in conflicts with one another (18:15–21; 24:10). Still others succumbed to teachings of false prophets (24:5, 11). Lively expectation and vibrant hope had given way to doubt, anxiety, disillusionment, and full engrossment in the cares of the world (13:22). Matthew's emphatic answer was sure to inspire and encourage those who asked: "Where is he?" Live in expectation! "Keep awake therefore, for you do not know on what day your Lord is coming" (24:42).

Real expectation includes persistent vigilance, like that practiced by the dutiful person who watches and stays awake at night to guard priceless valuables. So Christians are to live in unremitting, confident, and joyous expectation of Christ's coming.

During the period of Noah, men and women languished in their expectation of God's reality and coming judgment (24:37–39). Likewise, in a tradition about two women and two men engaged in similar occupations, one person in each pair was taken and one was left (24:40–41). The Matthean parallelism highlights his pastoral theme: expectation and preparedness in daily living are essential for Christian men and women.

Matthew 24:42–44 contains a graphic narration of a man whose house had been broken into because he was not awake and watching (24:43). The Greek *dioruchthenai*, "be broken into," refers to a thief who digs through the sun-dried brick wall of a typical Palestinian home to gain entrance. A watchful householder would have been living in vigilant expectation.

Matthew's comforting exhortation to a community struggling to live a moral life faithful to the coming of Christ represents a stirring challenge for Christians today. Christians are to experience and exhibit God's reign and fulfill God's will until Christ's return, using their time and gifts responsibly toward others (25:31–46). We are called to live in expectation.

Respond to the Word

- What preparations will your church make this week to anticipate Jesus' coming?
- What changes will you make this week so as to be better prepared for Jesus' coming?

Go with the Word

Waiting in Wonder

> *God of wonder and surprises*
> *we, who are full of expectation,*
> *wait in hope of the promises*
> *of this season of gladness.*
>
> *Christ, whose birth was foretold*
> *by prophets full of wisdom*
> *and words of challenge and comfort,*
> *we trust in the promise of your coming.*
>
> *Holy Spirit, by your power*
> *Mary, who was full of grace,*
> *became Mother of the Christ child,*
> *waiting on God in prayerful expectation.*
>
> *Eternal One, we look up from our everyday worries*
> *as we wait in hope of your holy birth—*
> *full of wonder and surprise—*
> *in us.*

From *The Inviting Word, Older Youth Learner's Guide* (Cleveland, Ohio:
United Church Press, 1995), 34. Used by permission.

A D r e a m o f P e a c e

The wolf shall live with the lamb, the leopard shall lie down with the kid, the calf and the lion and the fatling together, and a little child shall lead them. The nursing child shall play over the hole of the asp, and the weaned child shall put its hand on the adder's den. They will not hurt or destroy on all my holy mountain; for the earth will be full of the knowledge of God as the waters cover the sea.

Isaiah 11:6, 8–9

Bible Reading: Isaiah 11:1–10

Additional Bible Readings: Psalm 72:1–7, 18–19
                                                       Romans 15:4–13
                                                       Matthew 3:1–12

Enter the Word

- What is your dream of peace for the world?
- Where do you need peace in your own life?

In the midst of the hustle and bustle of Advent we read Isaiah's vision of peace. The prophet's poetic words give a sense of peace even in a world that is vastly different from the one in which the original audience lived.

Find a comfortable place to sit and try to envision peace in

today's world and peace in your own life. Then read Isaiah
11:1–10. Look back over the words and identify the phrases or
images that are the most powerful for you. As Christians, we
believe that this Messiah, who was to usher in the reign of peace,
has already come in the person of Jesus. Claim the peace that Jesus
offers to you.

As you encounter the additional readings, note that Psalm 72 is
a prayer of blessing for a ruler. Romans 15:4–13 looks at Jesus the
servant, who brought the gospel of peace for both Jews and
Gentiles. Matthew 3:1–12 recounts the work of John the Baptist as
he helped people prepare for the Messiah's coming.

> *Bringer of Peace, fill my heart with your peace that passes
> all understanding. Amen.*

Engage the Word

- How would Isaiah's prophetic words have helped his trou-
  bled society envision God's peace?

Isaiah, the great eighth-century prophet who was active in the
Kingdom of Judah (746–700 B.C.E.), was also passionately involved
in the social, political, and religious affairs of his time. His visions,
oracles, and prophecies provide historical snapshots of Israel's internal and external struggles, wars, triumphs, and hopes.

Isaiah 11:1–10 is set within the literary context of a series of
oracles against Judah (Isaiah 1–12). In spite of Isaiah's strong warn-
ings and admonitions for Judah to avoid alliances and involvement
with the great, pagan nation of Assyria, Judah had followed the
lead of her ruler King Ahaz in making a political alliance with
Assyria (2 Kings 16:7–20).

A disastrous consequence of Judah's political marriage with
Assyria was that Judah became a vassal state of the Assyrian
Empire, with King Ahaz allowing Assyria's native pagan practices,
cults, and superstitions to flourish in Judah (Isaiah 2:5–8; 8:19f).
Worship and obedience to God waned. Assyria's demands for trib-
ute meant that Ahaz was even obliged to empty the treasury and
strip the Temple in order to raise it (2 Kings 16:8, 17). In addition
to external problems, Israelite society suffered from within—the
wealthy oppressed the poor, and the notion that God's demands

could be met by ritual and sacrifice alone was widespread (Isaiah 1:10–17, 21–23; 28:7).[1]

Judah's desire for political independence and social and religious reform intensified over time. Many of Isaiah's oracles echo the eager longing for a better ruler, an ideal Davidic ruler who would establish a reign of justice and peace.

Isaiah 11:6, 8–9, sounds a note of hope! A righteous ruler will spring forth from the root of the Davidic family (11:1). He will be blessed with the Spirit of wisdom and understanding; he will render justice and righteousness throughout the land; and most of all, this ruler will delight in the knowledge and fear of God (Isaiah 11:1–5). Christians have always affirmed that Isaiah's oracles about the future king who would establish righteousness in the earth were fulfilled in Jesus of Nazareth.[2]

Isaiah 11:6, 8–9 provides a graphic and stunning vision of the realization of peace, restoration, and harmony that occurs in the entire created order when God's Righteous Ruler fully establishes the future that God has prepared for creation. The dominion of God's peace—*shalom*—recalls the serenity of Paradise.

The pastoral tranquillity in Isaiah 11:6, 8–9, depicts peace between domesticated animals and their natural predators. Coexistence and association marked by calm rest and peaceful grazing are real. Men and women also experience the conciliatory effects of God's reign on earth.

Christians in every age have anticipated the realization of Isaiah's vision of God's created order as fully renewed and restored. The Apostle Paul and the writer of Revelation heralded this hope in their own day (Romans 8:18–25; Revelation 21:1). The God of creation and history will establish peace in the earth through a redeemed creation.

Respond to the Word

- What can you do, alone or with a group, to bring about the justice and peace that Isaiah envisioned?
- What will you do to become more at peace with yourself?

Go with the Word

C. Terry Saul, *Tree of Jesse*, The Heard Museum, Phoenix, Arizona.
Used by permission.

    C. Terry Saul paints the ancient Hebrew prophecy of Isaiah from his Chickasaw/Choctaw world view. The Promised One is born of the Spirit, cradled in the arms of Mary, nurtured by branch after branch, by elder after elder that preceded him. The tree of Jesse leads to Isaiah's vision of peace within all of creation.

1. John Bright, *A History of Israel* (Philadelphia: The Westminster Press, 1972), 276.

2. Otto Kaiser, *Isaiah 1–12*, The Old Testament Library (Philadelphia: The Westminster Press, 1972), 162.

The Desert Blossoms

The wilderness and the dry land shall be glad, the desert shall rejoice and blossom; like the crocus it shall blossom abundantly . . . . Say to those who are of a fearful heart, "Be strong, do not fear! Here is your God. God will come with vengeance, with terrible recompense. God will come and save you."

Isaiah 35:1–2a, 4

Bible Reading: Isaiah 35:1–10

Additional Bible Readings: Psalm 146:5–10
                                   or Luke 1:47–55
                                   James 5:7–10
                                   Matthew 11:2–11

Enter the Word

- What might the image of a blossoming desert mean in relation to one's spiritual life?
- Where in your own life do you need to experience renewal?

As you read Isaiah 35:1–10 note the images these verses create. New life emerges from a barren and dry desert; new power comes to those who lacked it. The return of God to the land of God's chosen people brings redemption and new life. Think about the images for a moment. Recall times when you have seen a barren place bloom or witnessed healing when all seemed lost. Think about the times God has entered your life bringing renewed hope.

Read verse 10 once more. This message is for you, a ransomed child of God by virtue of the death and resurrection of Jesus Christ. God will again restore creation even as God continues to create. Advent not only suggests that God will send a Messiah but also speaks to our understanding of the final coming of Christ. We celebrate God's restoring and saving power in that fact.

Luke 1:47–55 is Mary's song of praise for God's salvation and mercy. Psalm 156:5–10 lifts praise for God's help. James 5:7–10 encourages us to wait patiently for God's coming. Matthew 11:2–11 shows Jesus performing works expected of the Messiah.

> *You who have the power to restore and save, enter my heart as I prepare for your coming. Amen.*

Engage the Word

- How might the prophet's words have given God's people hope?

Judah, Israel's southern kingdom, yearned to experience God's saving and restoring power. The Edomites, blood relatives of the Israelites, had long had a bitter hatred toward Israel. The belief that Judah and the Edomites were "blood-relatives" is traced to the story of Jacob and Esau. Esau was the father of the nation of Edom, making the Edomites relatives of the Israelites (Genesis 25, 27, 36:1, 8, 19).[1] Saul, David, Solomon, Amaziah, and Azariah had fought and dominated the Edomites (Obadiah 1–21; Jeremiah 49:7–22; Psalm 137). The prophet Amos charged Edom with the transgression of having "pursued his brother with the sword and cast off all pity" (Amos 1:11). The "brother" is presumed to be Judah (see Genesis 25, 27, 36:1, 8, 19).[2] The prophet Ezekiel also records that Edom had acted vengefully against the house of Judah and that God will stretch out God's hand against Edom (Ezekiel 25:12–14).

Both Judah and Edom had been dominated and ruled by the mighty Assyrian Empire during the eighth and seventh centuries B.C.E. But when the Babylonians crushed the Assyrians and fell heir to the empire (609 B.C.E.), Edom then became an ally of Babylon. In fact, when Babylon stormed Jerusalem's walls in 587 B.C.E., Edom encouraged the army's raging devastation, standing by as a pleased spectator (Psalm 137:7).

Isaiah 34:1–35:10 recounts the story of Edom's curse and Judah's renewal. God's retribution against Edom was sure and swift. God's unmistakable intervention on behalf of Judah effected a startling renewal and restoration of both the people and their land.

The title of the lesson, "The Desert Blossoms," must be understood against the backdrop of Judah's history of struggle and betrayal by Edom. Edom's intense persecution of Judah, which included menacing forays against Judah's already breached borders, made annual pilgrimages to Jerusalem quite dangerous for Judah's faithful worshipers. The motif of pilgrimage, first mentioned in Isaiah 2:2–4, recurs here in Isaiah 35:1–10. Edom's pressure created devastation and upheaval in the land and fear in the hearts of Judah's inhabitants. But God would restore Zion with saving and renewing power. God would bring life out of death.

The imagery in Isaiah 35:1–10 pulsates. The whole creation will participate in God's acts of restoration. The inhospitable terrain of the desert will be set free from its fruitless existence, rejoicing and blossoming abundantly. It will become a fruitful oasis with flowing, full streams of water, verdant vegetation, and brilliant flower fields. The ill, the infirm, and the fearful will be joyously set free, seeing with their own eyes the glory of God, the majesty of their God (35:2c). Pilgrims will travel the highway (the "Holy Way," 35:8) to Zion, singing and with everlasting joy.

God's good news for Judah is instructive for Christians today. God, who restores and saves with power, can transform the deserts of trial and suffering into places of rejoicing and renewal. God can make deserts bloom and fill them with peace and rejoicing.

Respond to the Word

- How can you help "the desert blossom" in the life of someone who is having a difficult time?
- Into what spaces of your own life will you allow God to bring renewal?

Go with the Word

The Desert Will Sing and Rejoice

The desert will sing and rejoice
and the wilderness will blossom with flowers;
and will see the Lord's splendor,
see the Lord's greatness and power.
Tell everyone who is anxious:
Be strong and don't be afraid.
The blind will be able to see;
the deaf will be able to hear;
the lame will leap and dance;
those who can't speak will shout.
They will hammer their swords into ploughs
and their spears into pruning-knives;
the nations will live in peace;
they will train for war no more.
This is the promise of God;
God's promise will be fulfilled.

Iona Community Worship Book (Glasgow, Scotland: Wild Goose
Publications, 1991). Copyright © 1991 Wild Goose Publications, Iona
Community. Used by permission.

---

1. See Lawrence Boadt's discussion of the history of the two nations in his *Reading the Old
Testament: An Introduction* (Mahwah, N.J.: Paulist Press, 1984), 48–49, 410–13.
2. Ibid., 410.

Name the Child Emmanuel

She will bear a son, and you are to name him Jesus, for Jesus will save the people from their sins. All this took place to fulfill what had been spoken by God through the prophet: "Look, the virgin shall conceive and bear a son, and they shall name him Emmanuel," which means, "God is with us."

Matthew 1:21–23

Bible Reading: Matthew 1:18–25

Additional Bible Readings: Isaiah 7:10–16/Psalm 80:1–7, 17–19
                                        Romans 1:1–7

Enter the Word

- What does a name say about parents' expectations for their child?
- If you could name yourself, what name would you choose? Why?

Read Matthew 1:18–25. If you have witnessed an infant baptism, try to recall the moment of naming the child. Consider the power given to identify another human being in name. To name a child is to claim that child as one's own, but many parents confess that a child truly belongs only to God. If adult baptism is the practice of your congregation, think of the moment at which the baptized claim their identity as children of God.

Speak your own name to yourself. If you know its meaning,

reflect on the ways your name identifies you and gives you power. Your family may have stories to tell about the gift of your name. Remember those stories. Remember your namesake, if you have one.

Matthew describes Joseph as a man who tried to do the right thing, first by the law, then by the word of God. Although he was to become the surrogate father of Jesus, Joseph knew God was the child's true parent. Matthew describes Jesus as Isaiah's promise fulfilled in the gift from God—a child who shall be called Emmanuel, "God with us."

Ponder the phrase "God with us." Think about the preparations made during Advent for the coming of this child. Think of the contrast between Joseph's first news of the birth and our preparations. An angel visited him in a dream and spoke of God's intervention in the events of his life. Think of the time when you first heard of the birth of Jesus.

Read the additional scriptures. Look for ways in which these readings reinforce ideas from today's reading in Matthew.

> *Open my heart that you, O God, may truly dwell in me. Amen.*

Engage the Word

- What significance would Matthew's community have attached to the story in Matthew 1:18–25, and especially to Jesus' name?

Matthew's story of the birth of Jesus, like Luke's, shows that Jesus' birth represented the fulfillment of promises made long ago in the Hebrew Scriptures (Luke 1:5–2:52; Matthew. 1:1–2:23). Joseph is a leading player in Matthew's account of the Messiah's advent. An angel instructs Joseph three times in a dream, charging him to take Mary as a wife (Matthew 1:20), to take Mary and Jesus to Egypt to flee Herod's persecution (2:13), and to return to the land of Israel, "for those who were seeking the child's life are dead" (2:19–20).

Matthew's community would have recognized immediately the significance of the angel's pronouncement: "Joseph, *son of David*, do not be afraid to take Mary as your wife, for the child conceived in her is from the Holy Spirit" (1:20; emphasis added). Joseph, who will name Jesus and become his legal father, is himself of Davidic descent, and Jesus thus belongs to a Davidic family (see also Luke 1:27; 2:4). For Matthew, Jesus' Davidic lineage fulfills the expectation of a messianic ruler.

As the angel of God explains to Joseph the epoch-making events about to unfold with Jesus' birth, the angel announces the significance of Jesus' name with unmistakable clarity: "You are to name him Jesus, for he will save his people from their sins" (1:21). "Jesus," the Greek form of the Hebrew "Joshua" (or *Yeshua*), means "Yahweh is salvation," or "God saves." Jesus Christ is named by God's command, the long-awaited Savior who redeems humanity from the guilt of sin. Jesus is the God who saves.

The restoring and saving power of Jesus' name unfolds further in his designation as "Emmanuel," which means "God is with us" (1:23). Matthew links Mary's chosen role as "the virgin through whom God becomes miraculously incarnate" to the young woman in Isaiah 7:10–16. Isaiah's prophecy was originally addressed to King Ahaz when Jerusalem was threatened during the Syro-Ephramite war (734–733 B.C.E.) (see also 2 Kings 16:1–20 and Isaiah 7:1–9). God promised to transfer the Davidic promises from faithless King Ahaz to another Davidic ruler, presumably Ahaz's son Hezekiah, soon to be born of his young wife Abijah. The implication is that the young girl of marriageable age would be a virgin (2 Chronicles 28:16–29:2).[1]

Matthew links the tradition of God's assuring presence with fearful Israel (Emmanuel, "God is with us," Isaiah 7:14) to the far more profound theological affirmation that Jesus is the very incarnation of God: Jesus *is truly* "Emmanuel," the God who abides with us in both presence and saving activity.

The angel's words surely prompt all to rejoice who see in these words God's unfathomable and loving determination to be born with us *for the sake of our salvation!*

Respond to the Word

- With whom can you share the good news that God is with us?
- How will God's presence in Jesus impact your life this week?

Go with the Word

O Come, O Come, Emmanuel

O Come, O come, Emmanuel,
And ransom captive Israel,
That mourns in lonely exile here,
Until the Child of God appear.
Rejoice! Rejoice!
Emmanuel shall come to you,
O Israel!

O come, O Wisdom from on high,
And order all things far and nigh;
To us the path of knowledge show,
And help us in that way to go.
Rejoice! Rejoice!
Emmanuel shall come to you,
O Israel!

. . .

O come, O Day-spring, come and cheer
Our spirits by your advent here;
Love stir within the womb of night,
And death's own shadows put to flight.
Rejoice! Rejoice!
Emmanuel shall come to you,
O Israel!

O Come, Desire of Nations, bind
All peoples in one heart and mind;
Make envy, strife, and quarrels cease;
Fill the whole world with heaven's peace.
Rejoice! Rejoice!
Emmanuel shall come to you,
O Israel!

Latin, ca. 9th century, trans. John M. Neale, 1851; sts. 1, 4 trans. Henry S. Coffin, 1916, alt.; in *The New Century Hymnal* (Cleveland, Ohio: The Pilgrim Press, 1995), 116. Used by permission.

1. See also George T. Montague, *Companion God. A Cross-Cultural Commentary on the Gospel of Matthew* (Mahwah, N.J.: Paulist Press, 1990), 21.

Giotto di Bondone, *Madonna and Child*, Uffizi, Florence, Italy
(Alinari/Art Resource, N.Y.). Used by permission.

Christmas

Weeks of waiting have finally ended. God's own self is revealed in a newborn babe carefully wrapped in swaddling cloths and tenderly laid in a makeshift cradle in the manger where he was born. The purity, innocence, and divinity of this blessed Child is symbolized by white, the liturgical color used in churches during the twelve days of the Christmas season.

God's own Word "became flesh and lived among us" (John 1:14a). Jesus' coming is indeed good news for the whole earth. Nothing will ever again be the same because God's reign has broken in upon the world in the person of Emmanuel. This is the One whom the prophets foretold would come as the Savior. All creation, including angels from on high and a star in the sky, herald the arrival of the Beloved Child sent as a gift from God to be the Messiah, the Anointed One, the Christ.

The light of the star is reflected in the myriad of lights adorning Christian homes, for Jesus is the light of the world. Look at the Coptic personal icon, *Virgin and Child*. Notice how the light of the World enlightens and enlivens all who encounter God's Beloved Child. Ponder how the light of Jesus' life has given you new life and hope. Consider the transforming effect that this child has upon humanity and creation itself.

Light Shines in the Night

All things came into being through God's Word, and without the Word not one thing came into being. What has come into being in the Word was life, and the life was the light of all people. The light shines in the night, and the night did not overcome it.

John 1:3–5

Bible Reading: John 1:1–14

Additional Bible Readings: Isaiah 52:7–10
                                    Psalm 98
                                    Hebrews 1:1–4 (5–12)

Enter the Word

- How is light an apt symbol for God's Word, Jesus?
- Where do you need light to shine in the shadows of your life?

If you study before daybreak or after sunset, light a candle or turn on a flashlight. Give thanks to God for this light that illuminates the shadows. Contemplate what human life would be like if there were no light.

Now read John 1:1–14, part of this gospel's Prologue. Consider how Jesus, God's enfleshed Word, is the light of your own life. Wrestle with the possibility that you are clinging to murky places in your soul that you do not want Jesus to enlighten. Name those places and turn them over to the One who comes "full of grace and truth" to bring you "grace upon grace" (1:14, 16).

As you read the additional scriptures, notice how they relate to

John's Prologue. Isaiah 52:7–10 speaks of messengers who announce the good news of salvation, just as John the Baptist proclaimed Jesus' coming. In Psalm 98 all creation is called to praise God, who will reign on earth with justice and righteousness. The writer of Hebrews 1:1–4 (5–12) tells us that Jesus, "the exact imprint of God's very being," sustains all things with his word.

> *Light of the World, dispel the shadows that surround me*
> *so that I may see you more clearly. Amen.*

Engage the Word

- According to John, what is the purpose of God's Word?

When we look at all four of the Gospels, we discover that Mark, the earliest one (written around 70 C.E.) begins the story of Jesus with his baptism. Matthew and Luke push the story back to Jesus' birth with genealogies traced to Abraham and Adam, respectively.

In John's Gospel, with words reminiscent of Genesis 1:1, the opening verse proclaims, "In the beginning was the Word" (1:1). The Word (*Logos*) of God, at work to create the world, now becomes the Word made flesh in the humanity of Jesus. The Creator, proclaimed in the Hebrew Scriptures as the creator of light (Genesis 1:3), now is present and at work as light in Jesus.

"What has come into being in the Word was life, and the life was the light of all people" (John 1:3b–4), "the true light, which enlightens everyone" (1:9). The theme of light here at the beginning of John's Gospel is also a theme elsewhere in this gospel (see 3:19–21, 8:12, 9:5, 11:9–10, 12:35–36). Jesus is "the light of the world," who illuminates and heals human life and is not overtaken by the night of the world (1:5).

For the readers of this gospel toward the end of the first century, John's partially hymnic Prologue (1:1–18) serves as a kind of overture to the rest of the gospel. The life and ministry, death and resurrection of Jesus that follow, prompt such words in the Prologue as life, light, believe, glory, grace, and truth. He is the life and light, grace and truth, whose glory (a word that point's to God's presence) calls for believing in him.

Further, words of prose in the Prologue about John the Baptist break the hymnic poetry to make sure the readers do not mistake

John as the light (note 1:6–8, 15; see also 1:19–20, 3:28–30). At that time, there still were those who saw John as the Christ, the Messiah. To help counter this view, in John's Gospel the disciples of John the Baptist become the first disciples of Jesus (1:35–42).

The major purpose of this gospel is to proclaim Jesus as Messiah and Child of God, to encourage believing in him, and to meet the challenge of those saying that he was not the Messiah: "Now Jesus did many other signs in the presence of his disciples, which are not written in this book. But these are written so that you may come to believe that Jesus is the Messiah, the Child of God, and that through believing you may have life in his name" (20:30–31).

The Prologue speaks of that world of persons who did not accept him (1:10–11), but it also proclaims that those who do receive him and believe in his name (that is, in the essence of everything he stands for) will be empowered to become God's children (1:12–13).

To believe in Jesus is to believe in that personal Word who "became flesh and lived among us" (literally, "tabernacled" among us) to show the presence of God's grace and truth, the grace and truth of God's self-giving love for the world (1:14, 3:16).

Words from Isaiah have a similar ring. God "has bared God's holy arm before the eyes of all the nations; and all the ends of the earth shall see the salvation of our God" (Isaiah 52:10; see also Psalm 98:1–3). Like John's Gospel, the Letter to the Hebrews ties God's Word in Jesus to creation and to God's glory and presence in him (Hebrews 1:2–3).

Respond to the Word

- How can your faith community let light shine for others?
- What areas of your own life will you ask God to illuminate?

Go with the Word

Christmas Litany

> *One: In the beginning was the Word,*
> *and the Word was with God*
>
> *Many: and the Word was God.*
>
> *One: In the beginning there was not light,*
>
> *Many: but the light of God shown in the shadows.*
>
> *One: God was the true light.*
>
> *Many: Jesus Christ, the Child of God,*
> *came as the light of the world.*
>
> *One: In the beginning was the Word,*
>
> *Many: and the Word dwelt among us.*
>
> *All: The Word became flesh full of grace and truth.*

Paraphrase of John 1:1, 5, 14, in *The Inviting Word Older Youth
Learner's Guide* (Cleveland, Ohio: United Church Press, 1995), 77.
Used by permission.

Gloria in Excelsis Deo

Praise God! Praise God from the heavens; praise God in the heights! Praise God, all God's angels; praise God, all God's host! Young men and women alike, old and young together! Let them praise the name of God for God's name alone is exalted!

Psalm 148:1–2, 12–13a

Bible Reading: Psalm 148

Additional Bible Readings: Isaiah 63:7–9
Hebrews 2:10–18
Matthew 2:13–23

Enter the Word

- Which songs of praise have filled the air recently?
- What reasons do you have for offering praise to God?

Read Psalm 148, a psalm of praise. Think back to Christmas Eve and Christmas Day. Recall the songs that made you feel the most joyous. Think about the moment when the good news of the birth was announced in the reading of the Christmas story. In Luke 2:14 angels' voices filled the sky and, in the words of the psalmist, praised God.

In the days that follow Christmas people often experience mixed emotions. Sometimes the joy of the moment seems to pass in the blink of an eye. For others there is relief that a hectic celebration is finally over. The glory of the birth announcement seems to fade quickly. It is sometimes hard to remember that Christmas lasts for twelve days. It is even harder to keep the joy of Christmas in one's heart for the month to come.

Yet the psalmist wrote this song without any knowledge of Christmas, only the knowledge of a God too glorious for words. The psalm gathers every image possible to convey a sense of the profound greatness of God. The one clear message is that everyone is to praise God forever.

You may not feel like praising God at this moment. This can be a taxing time of year. But take the challenge: read Psalm 148 one more time and try to let the words encourage you and invite God to fill you with joy.

God is known in creation—in every snowflake, every raindrop, every glistening ray of sunshine—and God is in you. Rejoice at the words of the psalm. Close your eyes and imagine all the earth celebrating the birth of the Savior. As you study the additional Bible readings, see how they too call us to praise God.

> *I join with all creation in praising you, O God, for your name alone is exalted. Amen.*

Engage the Word

- How does the psalmist imagine all creation praising God?

"Praise God!" Psalm 148 begins and ends emphatically with thunderous exuberance in this resplendent refrain. The intervening verses, framed by the call to praise Yahweh, show unmistakably that the praise of God is the goal of all creation.

Psalm 148 is a celebratory hymn that glorifies God as Creator and Redeemer. While the psalm was composed at a particular (though unknown) place and time in history, the scope of the psalmist's vision of those invited to join in the resounding praise of God is universal and eternal. Verses 1–6 beseech the heavenly world to praise God. The psalmist attempts to name the farthest reaches of the universe by identifying spatial limits from which the praise should proceed: "Praise God from the heavens; praise God in the heights!" (Psalm 148:1). Celestial beings, too, with the sun, moon, and stars, are to praise their Creator, for God had commanded, and they were created (148:5).

Earthly creatures, too, proclaim the unsurpassed majesty of

their Creator. Verses 7–12 present a carefully detailed and wide-ranging enumeration of created things and beings that are invited to join the sonorous choir of praise, including meteorological phenomena (fire, hail, snow, frost, wind), vegetation, wild and domesticated animals, creeping and flying animals. The very earth—the majestic mountains and the humble hills—offers its privileged witness of adoration to its Maker. The entire created order that God declared "in the beginning" (Genesis 1:1) to be "very good" (Genesis 1:31) now returns its "Hallelujahs" to its Creator with inexhaustible praise.

It is no accident that the psalmist's list of created earthly phenomena in verses 7–12 reaches its climax in verses 11–12 with the creation of humankind. The psalmist David had also declared that God crowned human beings uniquely with glory and honor (Psalm 8:3–5).

Psalm 148:12–13a highlights the inclusive character of the global human community that praises and worships the Creator. They are men and women, young and old. And they are "together" (148:12) in this praise, in community, in harmony.

How appropriate for all creation to praise God during this Christmas season! The Latin phrase *gloria in excelsis Deo*, translated "Glory to God in the highest," originates in Luke 2:14. In Greek it is *doxa en hupsistois Theo*. An angel of God announced good news of great joy to shepherds out in the field. A heavenly host joined the angel, praising God (Luke 2:13–14).

Other Bible readings for today remind us that God is to be praised for God's own praiseworthy acts (Isaiah. 63:7–9) and for God's indescribable gift of Jesus Christ (Hebrews 2:10–18). Let everything that has breath praise God! Gloria in excelsis Deo!

Respond to the Word

- During this Christmas season, how will you join with others to praise God, especially for the gift of the Christ Child?
- What do you see, hear, taste, touch, or smell that calls you to praise God? How will you respond?

Go with the Word

Born in the Night, Mary's Child

Born in the night, Mary's Child, a long way from Your home;
Coming in need, Mary's Child, born in a borrowed room.

Clear shining light, Mary's Child, Your face lights up our way;
Light of the world, Mary's Child, dawn on our darkened day.

Truth of our life, Mary's Child, You tell us God is good;
Yes, it is true, Mary's Child, shown on your cross of wood.

Hope of the world, Mary's Child, You're coming soon to reign;
King of the earth, Mary's Child, walk in our streets again.

God in the Flesh

And the Word became flesh and dwelt among us full of grace and truth.

John 1:14a, c

Bible Reading:	John 1:(1–9), 10–18
Additional Bible Readings:	Jeremiah 31:7–14/ Psalm 147:12–20 Ephesians 1:3–14

Enter the Word

- What feelings and meanings come to mind when you read the words "God in the flesh"?
- How did the Word—God in the flesh—enter your life this Christmas?

Read John 1:1–18. The author of John's Gospel talks of God's power to create from the beginning moments. Think of the beginning of time and the entrance of Jesus Christ as God's active agent in the creation of life. Recall a time when you entered a shadowy room and turned on the light, or perhaps lit a candle. When light enters a void you are able to see all you could not see before. In the reading from John, the birth of Jesus is noted as a time when light entered the world. Jesus is called the "true light" (John 1:9).

John says that when Jesus entered this world he became the embodiment of the Word—he "became flesh and lived among us" (1:14). Jesus, the living Word, was full of grace and truth.

Ponder ways that the Word entered your life this season. Perhaps you participated in a pageant or sang carols with the congregation or choir. Maybe the Word entered your heart through the laughter of children or the reminiscing of older people. If you have not yet found time to be alone with the Word, take time now.

Read the John text again and try to visualize the powerful imagery of John's poetic style. If you have time, sing or speak the words of a favorite Christmas carol and think of how you have shared Christmas with others in the past. Reflect on the most pleasant memory you can recall.

Turn now to the additional readings. Jeremiah 31:1–14 speaks of the future homecoming of the dispersed exiles as they return to Israel. God who is loving and faithful will fulfill this promise. Psalm 147:12–20 sings praises for God's power and care. Ephesians 1:3–14 offers words of praise and thanksgiving for God's blessings.

> *I praise you, O God, for in Jesus, your Incarnate Word, you have made yourself known to me. Amen.*

Engage the Word

- How does John's story of Christ's coming differ from that of Matthew and Luke?

One writer has observed that "Christmas is a gift of love wrapped in human flesh and tied securely with the strong promises of God."[1] Nearly two thousand years ago (90–100 C.E.), the writer of John's Gospel celebrated similar good news with members of his community: God's gift of love was revealed in the incarnation of Jesus, "God in the Flesh." Christians still celebrate the inexhaustible truth of John's good news with joyous thanksgiving today.

With John's witness to the Incarnation, we continue the story of the mighty in-breaking of God's dominion and the historical significance of Jesus. John's story unfolds in the prologue of the Gospel (John 1:1–18), which are among the most significant verses in the New Testament. Like the overture to a great opera, these eighteen verses present an introduction of God's unique self-disclosure in Jesus, with an outline of the significance of this self-disclosure for all creation.

Grasping the profundity of such a familiar biblical text as John 1:1–18 today may be challenging for some readers. Its familiarity may have caused some to become "dulled" to its timeless importance, resulting in a kind of "domestication" of its resplendent message. All of us need to see and grasp anew its wonderful truths for faith and life.

John seeks to convey the profundity and majesty of God's self-disclosure in God's only Child so that all may truly know and believe in God and become children of God (1:10–13).

The Word is now incarnate in Jesus, preexistent and an active, living personality (1:1–2). Moreover, the Word is deity: "and the Word was God" (1:1). The Word creates and illumines life (1:3–5, 9).

To remember and celebrate the birth of Jesus at Christmas is to recall that God freely chose to become incarnate out of love for us. John's powerful and memorable words—"And the Word became flesh and lived among us, full of grace and truth" (1:14)—would serve to remind his community that their very creation and life were the result of their faith in the Incarnate One.

John's climactic words in today's Bible reading affirm that the nature and character of the invisible God are interpreted by and can be seen in God's only Child, who is uniquely qualified to interpret God, for the only Child is close to God's heart (1:18). In Jesus, the "invisible" God became a part of the visible world.

During this Christmas season, may all celebrate the wonderful reality that God's great mercy, grace, and love have come to all in Jesus Christ.

Respond to the Word

- In what ways will you seek to know God more fully through the Incarnate Jesus?
- How can you bring "God in the Flesh" to someone else this week?

Go with the Word

*You have come
to us as a small child,
but you have
brought us the greatest
of all gifts, the gift
of eternal love.
Caress us with your
tiny hands, embrace us
with your tiny arms,
and pierce our hearts with
your soft, sweet cries.*

Bernard of Clairvaux, in *The HarperCollins Book of Prayers: A Treasury of Prayers through the Ages*, compiled by Robert Van de Weyer (San Francisco: HarperSan Francisco, 1993), 64.

1. Carlton C. Buck, "What Is Christmas?" *The Minister's Manual,* ed. Charles L. Wallis (1980 ed; New York: Harper and Row, 1979), 59.

Adoration of the Magi, detail, from the tomb of Archbishop Dietrich II
von Moers, 15th century, Cologne Cathedral, Cologne, Germany
(Foto Marburg/Art Resource, N.Y.). Used by permission.

Epiphany

During the season of Epiphany, Jesus' identity becomes clear as he is made known to the world. Epiphany begins on January 6, the twelfth day of Christmas. The word "epiphany," which means manifestation or disclosure, is often associated with the story of the Magi who recognize the significance of the birth and journey from the East to worship the Child. In the remaining weeks that precede Lent, Jesus' identity is further revealed as John baptizes him in the Jordan, as he begins his public ministry by turning water into wine at the wedding in Cana, and as he is brilliantly transfigured on the mountain in the presence of his close friends Peter, James, and John.

Throughout most of the season, the green of ordinary time is used. However, the celebrations of Epiphany, the Baptism of Jesus, and the Transfiguration are marked by celebratory white altar cloths.

Look at the detail, *Adoration of the Magi*, from a German tomb. Imagine yourself as each one of these kings who has come to adore Jesus. Think about why you have sought out Jesus. Reflect on the gift that you are bringing. What does it symbolize for you? How do you hope it will be received?

Now envision yourself kneeling before Jesus. Why have you come seeking Jesus? What gifts do you bring? How can you help others to recognize who Jesus is?

God Plays No Favorites

Then Peter began to speak to them: "I truly understand that God shows no partiality, but in every nation anyone who fears God and does what is right is acceptable to God. You know the message God sent to the people of Israel, preaching peace by Jesus Christ—Christ is Lord of all."

Acts 10:34–36

Bible Reading: Acts 10:34–43

Additional Bible Readings: Isaiah 42:1–9/Psalm 29
                                      Matthew 3:13–17

Enter the Word

- How is the message that God plays no favorites good news?
- With whom do you play favorites? Why?

Take your Bible and find a comfortable place for study. Close your eyes and remember a time when you observed or experienced the consequences of someone's "playing favorites." What was the basis for the favoritism? Recall how this exercise of partiality affected those who benefited from it and those excluded by it.

Think about times in your life when you played favorites with friends, with family members, with co-workers, and/or with members of your church community. Why did you act partially? Ponder how your favoritism affected your relationships with those involved.

Turn to Acts 10. Skim verses 1–33, which lead up to today's

text. Notice Peter's anxiety. Notice also how God addresses this anxiety to prepare the apostle for ministry.

Read Acts 10:34–43, focusing on the consequences of God's impartiality (i.e., acceptableness to God, forgiveness of sins) declared in principle by Peter's opening words in 10:34. Think back on your own experiences of favoritism and about the ways in which those experiences would have been different if you (or others) showed no partiality. Examine your own life to see places where God is calling you to set aside prejudice.

Recall the words of a children's song and its familiar phrasing of the principle underlying Peter's declaration:

Jesus loves the little children,
All the children of the world;
Red and yellow, black, brown, white,
They are precious in his sight;
Jesus loves the little children of the world.

Turn now to the additional readings. Isaiah 42:1–9, which includes the first Servant Song, declares God as the creator of all who provides for all. Psalm 29 is a hymn to God who speaks in the storm. Matthew 3:13–17 is this gospel writer's account of Jesus' baptism by John.

> *Search me, O God, and cleanse me of the partiality*
> *I show to others. Amen.*

Engage the Word

- What response might Luke's Gentile audience have had to the news that God plays no favorites?

Some of the popular religious movements in the Greco-Roman world of the first century "played favorites." They had strict rules about who could become "members." Mithraism, based on the worship of the sun-god Mithra and a strong rival of Christianity, forbade the admission of women to the cult. Cynicism, one of the philosophical movements in the Roman Empire, advanced a teaching prescribing that the highest virtue was to have no wants at all. The abandonment of most societal conventions, including the securing of wealth, attracted certain types of devotees to their philosophical system.[1]

Luke, the writer of Acts, proclaims wonderful news in Acts 10:34–43: "God plays no favorites." God's divine plan for the salvation of humankind through Jesus Christ is available to all: men, women, and children; young and old, from every race and nation.

Acts 10:34–43 is part of a tradition that records Peter's struggle to understand that God brings salvation in Jesus Christ to the whole world, Jew and Gentile alike. The first Christians were Jews who were convinced that God's covenant was for the Jews only. The Christians who gathered together in the upper room, awaiting the outpouring of the Holy Spirit, were Jews (Acts 1:6–2:21). Acts 1–7 focuses largely on the life and ministry of Christian Jews in Jerusalem. With the conversion of the God-fearing Cornelius in Acts 10, Peter finally understood that "God shows no partiality, but in every nation anyone who fears God and does what is right is acceptable to God" (10:34–35). The stage now is set for the full-scale launching of the Gentile mission.

"God plays no favorites." This means that the church has no place for discrimination based on economic class, gender, or national heritage. Both Lydia, the wealthy businesswoman, and the less prosperous Philippian jailer were recipients of the church's ministry (see Acts 16:11–15, 25–34). Women were disciples and leaders empowered by God's Spirit, and with their brothers in Christ were persecuted for their faith (read Acts 1:14; 8:1–3; Romans 16:1–16). The church in Acts mirrored the global mosaic of persons that God welcomed into the heavenly fellowship: Jews, Greeks, Samaritans, Africans, and all others.

Luke presents Peter's words in Acts 10:34–43 as a sermon. This little sermonic treatise provides a wonderful summation of God's welcome of all persons to the table (see Luke 14:12–24). All are truly welcome, for "God plays no favorites."

Respond to the Word

- How can your church be more open so as to include all persons?
- What changes will you begin to make this week to be more inclusive and welcoming in your personal relationships?

Go with the Word

Almighty God,
as your Son our Savior
was born of a Hebrew mother,
but rejoiced in the faith of a Syrian woman
and of a Roman soldier,
welcomed the Greeks who sought him,
and suffered a man from Africa to carry his cross,
so teach us to regard [all faithful people] as
fellow-heirs of the kingdom of Jesus Christ. . . .
Amen.

Toc H. as quoted in *The Oxford Book of Prayer* (London: Oxford
University Press, 1985), no. 218, alt.

1. Merrill C. Tenney, *New Testament Times* (Grand Rapids: William B.
Eerdmans, 1975), 117.

What Are You Seeking?

The next day John again was standing with two of his disciples, and as he watched Jesus walk by, he exclaimed, "Look, here is the Lamb of God!" The two disciples heard him say this, and they followed Jesus. When Jesus turned and saw them following, he said to them, "What are you looking for?"

John 1:35–38a

Bible Reading: John 1:29–42

Additional Bible Readings: Isaiah 49:1–7/Psalm 40:1–11
1 Corinthians 1:1–9

Enter the Word

- What do you think many people are seeking today?
- What are you looking for in your own life?

On a sheet of paper list all the names or titles you have heard used in reference to Jesus. Recall names you have heard in scripture readings, prayers, and hymns. Then circle those titles that express who Jesus is in your life. Ponder how each of these understandings of who Jesus is affects your prayer life, your daily practice of faith, and your choice of congregations.

Read John 1:29–42. Write down the titles you find in that passage that refer to Jesus. Ponder what those titles reveal about the character and/or mission of Jesus. Compare the gospel writer's titles for Jesus with those that you have on your list.

92

Reread John 1:38a. Flip your paper over and at the top of the page, write Jesus' question: "What are you looking for?" On the left side of the paper under the question, write "life." Make notes that describe what you want out of life for yourself—personally, spiritually, vocationally. On the right side of the paper write "church" and jot down words or phrases that summarize what you want from your congregation.

Now reread the titles of Jesus that you circled earlier and consider how your understanding of Jesus' identity influences what you want from life and your church.

Also read the passages from Isaiah, Psalm 40, and 1 Corinthians and try to relate them to the message in John.

> *I seek you, O God, with all my heart and know that you are with me. For your presence I give you thanks. Amen.*

Engage the Word

- How would the gospel writer's presentation of Jesus have helped his community recognize Jesus for who he is?

The Gospel of John was written toward the end of the first century. The writer of John did not provide a simple report about Jesus (a church history), but he wrote theological proclamation.

Since members of John's community did not have physical proof of Jesus' existence, John writes to inspire and renew their faith in Jesus as the Christ and Child of God. The writer makes this theological purpose explicit in John 20:30–31: "Now Jesus did many other signs in the presence of his disciples, which are not written in this book. But these are written so that you may come to believe that Jesus is the Messiah, the Child of God, and that through believing you may have life in his name."

The story of the call of the first disciples in John's Gospel unfolds with graphic clarity. What appears to be an ordinary dialogue between Jesus and two followers of John the Baptist is imbued with significance, for it provides us with a picture of two followers eager to recognize Jesus for who he is.

As Jesus walks by him, John the Baptist exclaims: "Look, here is the Lamb of God!" (John 1:36; see also 1:29). The followers of John the Baptist, Andrew and the unnamed disciple (see John

1:40—many scholars believe this is John the disciple), immediately detected great significance in the Baptist's stirring declaration. Curious and eager to know about this person so recognized by John the Baptist, they followed Jesus, wanting to know who he was.

Jesus saw them following him, turned, and asked them: "What are you looking for?" (1:38). The question illustrates two points. First, Jesus recognized their presence, their curiosity, their interest. And second, Jesus took the initiative in meeting them halfway. His words invited a response from them, opening the door to further dialogue.

Jesus' question represents a marvelous example of divine initiative. Members of John's community learned an illuminating truth from the tradition of Jesus' call of the first disciples: When human beings begin to seek God, when men and women want to know and recognize Jesus for who he is, God meets them. They are invited to "draw near" and to follow Jesus on the road of life.

Jesus' pointed question: "What are you looking for?" reminds all who follow Jesus that they are to clarify their motives for following him. The two disciples stated that they wished to know where Jesus stayed, an indication that they wanted more than a passing acquaintance with him (1:38). Tarrying with Jesus that day, they recognized him for who he was. Excitement in discovering the Messiah (the "Anointed," 1:41), prompted Andrew to find his brother, Simon Peter, to share the good news with him and to bring Simon Peter to Jesus (1:41–42).

The writer of John's Gospel reminds the members of his community that following Jesus, tarrying with him, and recognizing who he is can lead to such a joyous comprehension of Jesus' significance that their lives will be transformed.

Respond to the Word

- How can you present Jesus to others so that they might know who he is?
- What changes do you need to make to find what you are seeking in life?

Go with the Word

The Lamb

> *Little Lamb, who made thee?*
>   *Dost thou know who made thee?*
> *Gave thee life and bid thee feed,*
> *By the stream & o'er the mead;*
> *Gave thee clothing of delight,*
> *Softest clothing wooly bright;*
> *Gave thee such a tender voice,*
> *Making all the vales rejoice!*
>   *Little Lamb who made thee?*
>   *Dost thou know who made thee?*
>
> *Little Lamb I'll tell thee,*
> *Little Lamb I'll tell thee!*
> *He is calléd by thy name,*
> *For he calls himself a Lamb:*
> *He is meek & he is mild,*
> *He became a little child:*
> *I a child & thou a lamb,*
> *We are calléd by his name.*
>   *Little Lamb God bless thee.*
>   *Little Lamb God bless thee.*

William Blake, "The Lamb," in *Prose and Poetry of William Blake* (New York: Doubleday, 1965), 8–9.

Trust in God

God is my light and my salvation; whom shall I fear? God

is the stronghold of my life; of whom shall I be afraid?

Psalm 27:1

Bible Reading: Psalm 27:1, 4–9

Additional Bible Readings: Isaiah 9:1–4
                                                      1 Corinthians 1:10–18
                                                      Matthew 4:12–23

Enter the Word

- Under what circumstances do people trust in God?
- For what do you need to trust God at this point in your life?

It is often easy to trust in God during happy times when things go smoothly. It is harder to trust God during hard times, such as when illness, unemployment, or natural disaster strike. It is human nature in cases like these to worry about insurance coverage, bill payments, or shelter. Today's lesson reminds us that God is present in good and bad times. God's sustaining power is available in any crisis.

Think about your greatest worries. They may concern finances, work, family, or other relationships. Write the words "Trust in God" on a sheet of paper. Underneath the words, write the one thing you most worry about. Tell yourself that you are giving the worry to God. You may not be able to give your worry away, but remind yourself that you do not have to handle it all by yourself. Put the paper somewhere you will see it.

Tomorrow, add another worry to the paper. Continue adding one worry a day, until you have given all your worries to God. Any time your worries threaten to overwhelm you, ask for God's help and support. Remind yourself that God is trustworthy and that you are not alone.

Isaiah 9:1–4 prophesies the coming reign of a righteous ruler who will lift oppression and end war. First Corinthians 1:10–18 speaks of divisions within the church at Corinth. Matthew 4:12–23 records Jesus' early ministry.

> *Strengthen my trust in you, O God, for you are my light and my salvation. Amen.*

Engage the Word

- How does the psalmist's description of God assure readers that God is indeed trustworthy?

Tradition ascribes Psalm 27 to David, the young shepherd boy who became one of Israel's most illustrious kings. This exuberant song of trust represents a stirring summons to "Trust in God."

The grounds for this secure and fearless trust are outlined with compelling clarity in Psalm 27:1: "God is my light and my salvation; whom shall I fear? God is the stronghold of my life; of whom shall I be afraid?"

The two nouns "light" and "salvation" are juxtaposed and are resplendent with theological significance. Both words function as a hendiadys, a literary term meaning that the nouns express in complementary fashion the same thing or event from two different viewpoints.

"God is my light." This phrase occurs only here in the Hebrew Scriptures. While God is called "the light of Israel" in Isaiah 10:17 and the "everlasting light" of the people in Isaiah 60:19, 20, here in Psalm 27:1 God is—in a movingly personal and reassuring way— the light of all who place their trust in God. In the presence of God's light, the shadows of fear must flee, the believer's soul finds repose.

"God is my salvation." God's mighty acts of saving deliverance are here affirmed with great exultation. The psalmist declares that even in the presence of "enemies all around me," there is no room for fear (Psalm 27:6). The psalmist's God is his salvation, but God also engages in saving deeds. God "hides" the needy one in a day of trouble, "conceals" the needy one under the cover of God's tent, and sets the needy one "high on a rock" (27:5). The joy of placing confident trust in such a trustworthy God prompts the psalmist to offer sacrifices to God with "shouts of joy" and to "sing and make melody to God" (27:6).

The psalmist employs yet a third image to witness to God's trustworthiness and to affirm God's active care for human persons—that of a "stronghold" (27:1). The term "stronghold" attests to God's ability to provide reassuring protection in a time of need.

The psalmist's words present an irrepressible witness to God's trustworthiness. Whether threats that precipitate fear come from without or within, all may trust in God, recognizing that God as "light, salvation, and stronghold" is actively and steadfastly near.

Do not overlook that the psalmist uses two rhetorical questions. With these questions ("Whom shall I fear?" and "Of whom shall I be afraid?"), the psalmist affirms that no human person can threaten or diminish the grounds for a daring and confident trust in the God who is at once "light," "salvation," and "stronghold" of life. The rhetorical questions are reminiscent of the one we hear echoed by the Apostle Paul many centuries later: "If God is for us, who is against us?" (Romans 8:31b).

Respond to the Word

- Whom can you assure that God is indeed "light, salvation, and stronghold"? How can you offer that assurance?
- How might your life be different if you put greater trust in God to care for you in all situations?

Go with the Word

I want to write about hospitals and not being able to sleep all night and 200 pills you have to take each day in a certain order because the really nasty-tasting ones you save for the end. And how strangers blithely mention people who have died around you. And how all you want when you're in the hospital is a hot shower and someone to muscularly wash your hair, put on talcum powder and change the sweaty sheets.

God I could go on.

Oh Donna, I can't say I'm losing it, but I sure do get scared sometimes. Also, I feel like a watched pot sometimes with people around me looking at me like I'm going to explode any minute. God, the patience and strength does really have to come from within and I've certainly gotten in touch with "within" this year, but it doesn't always seem to be there. It's a mighty lesson I'm going through I feel, and you know what? There's no doubt I'm up to the challenge: I've got the strength, physically and certainly mentally. I really know that this AIDS scare is really just asking me to finally admit that I'm a lovely, wonderful human being. A source of joy— and the more I realize that, the better and calmer I'll feel. So there.

God, this makes sense, I think maybe that's what crises are for—to get us to realize and appreciate our worth.

William Dean Clark, unpublished letter of January 26, 1993. Used by permission of Anderson Clark. Bill died on February 12, 1993, in Graduate Hospital, Philadelphia.

What God Requires

God has told you, O mortal, what is good; and what does God require of you but to do justice, and to love kindness, and to walk humbly with your God?

Micah 6:8

Bible Reading: Micah 6:1–8

Additional Bible Readings: Psalm 15
1 Corinthians 1:18–31
Matthew 5:1–12

Enter the Word

- In what ways does God make divine expectations known?
- What do you think God requires of you personally?

All persons, regardless of their age, function better when they know the expectations placed upon them. Clear expectations make decisive choices possible. Micah 6:1–8 offers you an opportunity to encounter and explore one of the Bible's most succinct statements of what God requires of us.

Reflect on what you consider God's expectations of you to be. Then write those expectations on paper.

After you finish writing, study the list. Put a star by entries that pertain to relationships or interactions with other persons ("you and neighbor"). Circle the entries that relate to devotional life or spiritual obligations ("you and God").

Now compare the two lists. Which list has more entries— "you and neighbor" or "you and God"? Ponder ways that you can bring these two lists into greater balance, if necessary. As you seek to do what God requires, try to identify areas of personal growth.

Read Micah 6:1–8. Focus on verse 8 and keep its message in mind as you review your list of expectations. Try to designate each entry as a "justice," a "kindness," or a "humble walk with God" and see what the results reveal.

Continue your study by reading Psalm 15, which asks who may be admitted into Temple for worship. The psalmist makes clear that those who worship are morally and ethically upright persons. In Paul's first letter to the church at Corinth, he proclaims Christ crucified as the way to salvation. Matthew 5:1–12, which is part of the Sermon on the Mount, sets forth Jesus' teachings known as the Beatitudes. These twelve verses provide much insight as to how Christ's followers are to live.

> *Empower me, O God, that I might be able to do justice,*
> *love kindness, and walk humbly with you. Amen.*

Engage the Word

- What situations in eighth century B.C.E. Judah evoked Micah's prophecies concerning God's expectations?

Micah, the eighth-century prophet, was not of noble descent; he was one of the "common people" from the village of Moresheth in southwestern Judah (Micah 1:1). Micah's humble origins may have fueled his passionate plea to the wealthy nobles of Judea to change their patterns of social and economic abuse of the peasantry. He wanted to remind them of what God required.

The landowners coveted and seized fields and houses, disrupting the lives of men, women, and children (2:1–9). The rulers did not practice justice; they engaged in cruel oppression (3:1–4).

But Micah's oracles and laments of judgment were not intended for the ruling elite only. He invited all of Israel to remember God's faithfulness and God's saving deeds of old (6:3–5). Using the language of the law court in chapter 6, he depicts God speaking as both prosecutor and judge in the appeal, employing such words and phrases as "plead your case" and "controversy" (6:1–2).

Micah reminds the Israelites that God's expectations of them are not new—God has already made known the divine will in the past: "God has told you, O mortal, what is good" (6:8). Micah calls his hearers to combine sincere worship with justice and kindness and to "walk humbly" with God (6:6–8).

For Micah, the litmus test of a healthy relationship with God lies in assessing how one's worship life combines with actions toward others. If a person does not combine faithful worship with the practice of justice and kindness, one does not pass the test. "Kindness," *hesed*, refers to a covenant relationship that finds its fulfillment in acts of mercy.

For the faithful and saving God, sincere worship and the practice of social justice are twin elements in the life of faithful believers. Right relationships with both God and the members of the community are essential.

Psalm 15, one of the scripture passages for today, sets forth the motif that what God requires of God's people is the practice of justice, kindness, and willing obedience to God. The requirements of admission to the Temple (abiding in God's tent) and dwelling on God's holy hill (Psalm 15:1) include conformity to an ethic characterized by the nurturing of fair-mindedness and conciliation and mutuality toward friends, neighbors, and those who fear God (15:2–5). All of life is to be integrated in submission to God.

Respond to the Word

- How can you, working with others, proclaim God's expectations so that change might come about?
- What one expectation of God can you identify in your own life and act on this week?

Go with the Word

Called as Partners in Christ's Service

Called as partners in Christ's service,
Called to ministries of grace,
We respond with deep commitment
Fresh new lines of faith to trace.
May we learn the art of sharing,
Side by side and friend with friend,
Equal partners in our caring
To fulfill God's chosen end.

Christ's example, Christ's inspiring,
Christ's clear call to work and worth,
Let us follow, never faltering,
Reconciling folk on earth.
Men and women, richer, poorer,
All God's people, young and old,
Blending human skills together
Gracious gifts from God unfold.

Thus new patterns of Christ's mission,
in a small or global sense,
Help us bear each other's burdens,
Breaking down each wall or fence.
Words of comfort, words of vision,
Words of challenge, said with care.
Bring new power and strength for action,
Make us colleagues, free and fair.

So God grant us for tomorrow
Ways to order human life
That surround each person's sorrow
With a calm that conquers strife.
Make us partners in our living,
Our compassion to increase,
Messengers of faith, thus giving
Hope and confidence and peace.

Shine!

Let your light shine before others.

Matthew 5:16b

Bible Reading: Matthew 5:13–20

Additional Bible Readings: Isaiah 58:1–9a (9b–12)/
                         Psalm 112:1–9 (10)
                         1 Corinthians 2:1–12 (13–16)

Enter the Word

- What causes people's lives to shine?
- How does your Christian witness shine for others to see?

Read Matthew 5:13–20. Picture yourself sitting with a huge crowd of people on the side of a hill listening to Jesus talk about the realm and sovereignty of God. Hear Jesus declare, "You are the salt of the earth. . . . You are the light of the world."

Jesus is saying that if you believe in God and in life everlasting, you are obliged to take that belief to others. If you believe, you can "season" the lives of others, as salt seasons food so that the believing is appealing to them. Faith in God can also empower you to be a beacon that shines through the dimness of life.

During a Sunday morning service it is easy to "shine" while worshiping with like-minded individuals in familiar surroundings. But that light needs to go beyond those walls. Christians are called to "shine" before all humanity. Ponder how and where you shine for Christ so that others may see him.

Sometimes the term "witnessing" makes believers uneasy. Most Christians want to express their faith, but don't want to be pushy about it. Some people are able to talk openly about God and their faith more easily than others. Nevertheless all Christians can be an example to others of how faith in God shapes lives. In fact, actions probably give a more lasting image of belief than do words. Therefore, think about witnessing as a way of living.

Consider your witness to the world. Just like one lit candle can pierce the darkness, one kind word to another person or one act of justice may be the first step in letting your light shine to the world. Picture a room that is without light. Then try to visualize how it will look as one, two, ten, fifty candles are lit. Now, think of yourself as lighting a candle in that room with every act of kindness, every thoughtful word, every deed done from the heart and out of love of God. Let your light shine!

As you read the additional passages from Isaiah, Psalm 112, and 1 Corinthians see how they may link to Matthew 5:16b.

> *Let me shine, Light of the World, so that others may see*
> *you reflected through the prism of my life. Amen.*

Engage the Word

- What impact might Jesus' teachings from the Sermon on the Mount have had on his hearers?

"Let your light shine before others" (Matthew 5:16b). This is one of Jesus' most succinct exhortations to the disciples in the Matthew. It contains no qualifiers about how they "should" or "ought to" be the light of the world. The declaration (*assumes* this reality and reiterates it with imperative force and incontrovertible conviction.

Earlier, the writer of Matthew had narrated traditions that interpreted Jesus as both a great light and the light of the nations (4:12–17). Similarly, Jesus' followers are to allow their light to be visible to the world.

The injunction to "let your light shine" is addressed to the corporate community of believers. The use of the plural form of the second person, personal pronoun "your" certifies that *all* Christians are in view here, not a select few who might be considered more "prominent" individuals. Moreover, the light is to shine—not to a private society or to a fellowship of like-minded persons (as sometimes occurred in some of the Greco-Roman mystery religions)—but to the whole world.

Effective Christian witness in the world, mediated through

"good works," will both reveal the character of God and prompt observers to glorify the God whom they cannot see (5:16).

In Matthew 5:14–15, the symbols of a "city built on a hill" and a "lamp" accentuate the sensibility of the church's fulfillment of its mission to be God's witness in the world. Just as a city set on a hill cannot be hidden but is in full view, so should the church recognize that its visibility provides a perennial opportunity for it to engage in faithful witness in a needy world.

Palestinian oil lamps were widely used in the first century. Usually fueled by olive oil, they varied in design and ornamentation. Whether they were placed in private houses, in public buildings, jutted from crevices in walls, or placed on lamp stands, their light was meant to be seen, to illuminate the shadows. "No one after lighting a lamp puts it under the bushel basket, but on the lampstand, and it gives light to all in the house" (5:15). Just as lights should shine in the service of those in a dwelling, so Christians are to shine as vital luminaries in the world.

The idea that women and men who fear God should function as lights in the world is mentioned in Psalm 112, one of the readings for this lesson. Within this context, the beneficiaries of the light of God's gracious, merciful, and righteous followers are a more narrowly circumscribed group—the "upright" (112:4–6). Like Christ's witnesses in Matthew 5:13–20, they too are not overcome by the gloom of the world, but make the blessedness of God's light and salvation a reality in the world.

Respond to the Word

- What can your congregation do to be a beacon in the community?
- What one step will you take this week to let your light shine?

Go with the Word

Give to Each of Us a Candle of the Spirit

Give to each of us a candle of the Spirit, O God,
  as we go down into the deeps of our being.
Show us the hidden things, the creatures of our dreams,
  the storehouse of forgotten memories and hurts.
Take us down to the spring of life,
  and tell each one of us our nature and our name.
Give us freedom to grow in order that we may each
  become that self,
  the seed of which you planted in us at our making.
Out of the deeps we cry to you, O God.

George Appleton, *One Man's Prayers* (London: SPCK, 1967). Used by permission of SPCK.

Growing in God

What then is Apollos? What is Paul? Servants through whom you came to believe, as God assigned to each. I planted, Apollos watered, but only God gave the growth. So neither the one who plants nor the one who waters is anything, but only God who gives the growth.

1 Corinthians 3:5–7

Bible Reading: 1 Corinthians 3:1–9

Additional Bible Readings: Deuteronomy 30:15–20/
                                   Psalm 119:1–8
                                   Matthew 5:21–37

Enter the Word

- What helps persons to grow in God?
- How have different persons enabled you to grow in faith?

Read 1 Corinthians 3:1–9. Paul uses the metaphor of planting and growth to illustrate how the words of faith may enter our hearts and souls. It is an exquisite image, especially because it reminds us of the Creator whose plan for creation included the Savior.

Remember a time when you planted a seed, nurtured it, and waited for it to grow. Now recall the people in your own life who nurtured God's seed in you, all those who helped and coached you so the seed of faith would grow and mature. Reflect for a few moments on each of these individuals. Give thanks for each one and the role that he or she played in your faith journey.

Turn to Psalm 119, one of today's additional readings. Read

verses 1 through 8 and give thanks for the word and law of God through which others have nurtured you. Also read Deuteronomy 30:15–20 and decide whether you will choose life or death, based on your willingness or unwillingness to obey God. Conclude by reading Matthew 5:21–37, an example of how the law is to be truly understood.

> *Gardener God, I give you thanks for those who have nurtured your seed in me and praise that you have graciously allowed that seed to grow and flourish. Amen.*

Engage the Word

- How did Paul address the problem of divisiveness in the Corinthian church to try to bring about a harmonious resolution?

In Paul's first letter to the church at Corinth (written in approximately 54–55 C.E.), he addressed a series of practical problems facing the Corinthian Christians. In 1 Corinthians 3:1–9, Paul sought to correct a false conception of Christian ministry: the notion that following particular servants of God provided the key to "growing in God."

Strategically, Paul begins the discussion with a "what" and not a "who": "What then is Apollos? What is Paul? Servants through whom you came to believe. . ." (1 Corinthians 3:5). By focusing on the *function* of these people in the community instead of features of their *person* or *personalities*, Paul shows that their significance lies in their function as servants of God, whose responsibility it is to nurture faith and growth.

Paul employs the familiar agricultural imagery of farm workers, fields, and crops to make his point. Apostles are servants, like farmers, with particular tasks to perform, and each will have his or her reward, whether they plant or water the crops (3:6, 8). The field (church) itself belongs to God ("you are God's field," 3:9), and of greatest significance is that it is God who gives the growth (3:7). Boasting about allegiance to the farmers (servants) is misguided. It is God who causes the increase!

Paul's message to the Corinthians stresses the complementary character of both his work and that of Apollos. They are neither competitors nor adversaries, antagonists, or enemies. God uses a variety of people with different vocations to help in the task of building up the church.

"The one who plants and the one who waters have a common purpose" (3:8). Like players on a baseball or football team or participants in any group endeavor, the people through whom God nurtures faith are co-laborers, partners seeking to achieve the same aim and purpose. Paul states this theme twice in verse 9. First, he shifts to the first person plural in describing his partnership with Apollos: "For *we* are God's servants (3:9a). Second, Paul and Apollos are described as "working together," *sunergos* (3:9b). This means that they cooperate with and help each other, functioning fully as a cooperative communion of believers.

The desirability and necessity of conciliation in the Christian community is echoed in Matthew 5:21–37, one of the Bible readings. Valuing and preserving the intimate ties of communion with one another may mean addressing the issue of one's anger with an "offender" (Matthew 5:21–24). Satisfactory settlement of grievances should take precedence over divisiveness and alienation.

Growing in God involves a recognition that members of the family of God's dominion need to *choose* to develop and strengthen bonds of mutuality and partnership with the diverse persons who comprise its members.

Respond to the Word

- Think of church groups or other organizations in your community that may act competitively to achieve worthwhile goals. What lessons from Paul's letter to the Corinthians might you share with them to bring about greater cooperation?
- What can you do this week to thank at least one of the persons who has nurtured your faith?

Go with the Word

Rex Goreleigh, *Planting*, 1943, Evans-Tibbs Collection of Afro-American Art, Washington, D.C. Used by permission.

Recall those who have nurtured God's seed of faith in you and give thanks.

You Have Heard It Said, But I Say . . .

"You have heard that it was said, 'An eye for an eye and a tooth for a tooth.' But I say to you, Do not resist an evildoer. But if anyone strikes you on the right cheek, turn the other also. You have heard that it was said, 'You shall love your neighbor and hate your enemy.' But I say to you, Love your enemies and pray for those who persecute you. Be perfect, therefore, as your heavenly Father and Mother is perfect."

Matthew 5:38–39, 43–44, 48

Bible Reading: Matthew 5:38–48

Additional Bible Readings: Leviticus 19:1–2, 9–18
Psalm 119:33–40
1 Corinthians 3:10–11, 16–23

Enter the Word

- What are some examples of common sayings in our society that contrast with Jesus' teachings?
- If you could ask Jesus about one of his teachings, which one would it be? Why?

"God helps those who help themselves." While sayings such as this are often invoked as if they are grounded in the authority of the Bible, they are in fact not biblically based. Jesus' teachings offer a corrective to many popular sayings, both in his day and in ours.

Read Matthew 5:38–48. Look for the formula, "You have heard that it was said . . . . But I say to you." Try to locate the original saying by using notes in a study Bible, a concordance, or information from "Engage the Word." Ponder how Jesus' teachings are different from the original quote. Meditate on how you can implement these teachings in your life. Be sure to read the additional scriptures.

> *Let me live the kind of healing, generous, holy life to which you call me through Jesus. Amen.*

Engage the Word

- How would Matthew's community have found Jesus' teachings different from teachings that were familiar to them?

The writer of the Gospel of Matthew was an early Christian teacher in the last quarter of the first century. He reflects an understanding of his task in the words of Jesus (Matthew 13:52), joining the "old" of his Hebrew Scriptures with the "new" in Jesus and the early church. His Gospel is a kind of manual for Christian education, helpfully structuring it for his audience to include five major blocks of Jesus' teaching (chapters 5–7, 10, 13, 18, 24–25), a kind of new *Pentateuch* ("five scrolls": Genesis-Deuteronomy) for his Jewish Christian readers.

One of those blocks is the Sermon on the Mount (Matthew 5–7), in which Jesus, like Moses earlier, becomes the new authoritative teacher from the Mount (see 5:1–2; 7:28–29). Therefore, though Jesus fulfills the earlier teaching ("the law and the prophets," 5:17), he goes beyond it: "You have heard that it was said . . . . But I say" (5:21, 27, 33, 38, 43).

Jesus goes beyond the former teaching on retaliation, "An eye for an eye and a tooth for a tooth" (e.g. Exodus 21:23–25, which intends to set just retaliatory limits), by breaking the cycle of violence with a new way of being and acting.

God's reign does not meet evil with evil but with a generosity that goes beyond the ways human society usually functions (see Matthew 5:39–42). Jesus as the authoritative agent of God's reign calls for an exuberant generosity to transform measured justice and reluctant giving into a new healing pattern in human relationships.

The reading from Leviticus (19:1–2, 9–18) also points toward a generosity of spirit in the treatment of the poor, the alien, and persons with disabilities. There is to be no stealing, no fraud, no injustice, no slandering, no wrongful profit. A holy God calls for holiness of life.

The reading from Psalm 119:33–40 prays for teaching and understanding God's ways, not the ways of selfish gain or vanity but of a goodness and right that give life.

In Matthew 5:38–48, Jesus also goes beyond the old teaching on love and hate, "You shall love your neighbor and hate your enemy." The first part of this is based on Leviticus 19:18. As to the second part, there are no such specific words in Hebrew Scripture, but hatred of the enemy erupts at many points (e.g., Psalm 137:7–9, 139:19–22, 140:9–10).

Again, Jesus breaks the cycle of hate and expands the circle of love to include the enemy (Matthew 5:44). He challenges the kind of prayers that ask for destruction of the enemy and calls people to pray even for those who persecute them (5:44; see 5:10–11).

What is the basis for doing this? It is the way God operates toward the evil and the good, toward the righteous and the unrighteous. To do likewise makes people God's children (Matthew 5:45). Loving only those who will return that love is not the way of God's reign (5:46–47).

The Greek word translated "be perfect" (teleios, Matthew 5:48) can be rendered "make it your goal." That goal is to love one's enemies because that is the character of God. Love is not a sentimental feeling. Love actively seeks the good for the enemy. Jesus the Messiah is the one who now can say this with authority.

In 1 Corinthians 3:11, Paul also lifts up Jesus. The apostle later asserts that "you belong to Christ, and Christ belongs to God" (3:22–23). To belong to God means to let God's holy, healing, generous, loving Spirit live and work in us as the holy temple of the living God (3:16).

Respond to the Word

- What teachings of Jesus will you share with others?
- How can you demonstrate God's love for an enemy this week?

Go with the Word

The Enemy—the "Extraordinary"

Here [in Matthew 5:43–48], for the first time in the Sermon on the Mount, we meet the word which sums up the whole of its message, the word "love." Love is defined in uncompromising terms as the love of our enemies. Had Jesus only told us to love our [brothers and sisters], we might have misunderstood what he meant by love, but now he leaves us in no doubt whatsoever as to his meaning.

The enemy was no mere abstraction for the disciples. They knew him only too well. They came across him every day. There were those who cursed them for undermining the faith and transgressing the law. There were those who hated them for leaving all they had for Jesus' sake. There were those who insulted and derided them for their weakness and humility. There were those who persecuted them as prospective dangerous revolutionaries and sought to destroy them. Some of their enemies were numbered among the champions of the popular religion, who resented the exclusive claim of Jesus. These last enjoyed considerable power and reputation. And then there was the enemy which would immediately occur to every Jew, the political enemy in Rome. Over and above all these, the disciples also had to contend with the hostility which invariably falls to the lot of those who refuse to follow the crowd, and which brought them daily mockery, derision, and threats. . . .

Christian love draws no distinction between one enemy and another, except that the more bitter our enemy's hatred, the greater his need of love. Be his enmity political or religious, he has nothing to expect from a follower of Jesus but unqualified love.

Dietrich Bonhoeffer, *The Cost of Discipleship*, 2d ed. (New York: Macmillan, 1959), 162–63, 164.

Consider the Lilies of the Field

Look at the birds of the air; they neither sow nor reap nor gather into barns, and yet your heavenly Father feeds them. Are you not of more value than they? And can any of you by worrying add a single hour to your span of life? And why do you worry about clothing? Consider the lilies of the field, how they grow; they neither toil nor spin, yet I tell you, even Solomon in all his glory was not clothed like one of these. So do not worry about tomorrow, for tomorrow will bring worries of its own. Today's trouble is enough for today.

Matthew 6:26–29, 34

Bible Reading: Matthew 6:24–34

Additional Bible Readings: Isaiah 49:8–16a
Psalm 131
1 Corinthians 4:1–5

Enter the Word

- What might nature teach us about God's care for all creation?
- How far are you willing to trust God?

After you read Matthew 6:24–34, make a list of the ordinary concerns that often occupy your mind. Maybe you worry about how you will pay the mortgage or afford braces for your children or save for retirement. Make another list of extraordinary concerns that confront you, such as serious illness or the prospect of job loss.

Reread Matthew 6:24–34. After the words "life more than" in verse 25, read aloud your list of concerns. Hear Jesus' words about God's care for creation as if he were speaking directly to you.

Also read passages from Isaiah, 1 Corinthians, and Psalm 131.

> *I confess that I worry about things you have promised to provide. Help me to trust in you, God. Amen.*

Engage the Word

•   How might Jesus' words have helped Matthew's readers?

Following last Sunday's text, today's reading is another passage from Jesus' Sermon on the Mount. For some introduction to Matthew's Gospel, see the first two paragraphs for Epiphany 7.

After teachings about almsgiving, prayer, and fasting (Matthew 6:1–18)—three essential elements in the heritage of both Jesus and Matthew's Jewish-Christian audience—and teachings about true treasure (6:19–21) as well as light and darkness (6:22–23), Jesus raises the issue of loyalty: "No one can serve two masters. . . . You cannot serve God and *mamona*" (riches, material wealth, 6:24).

This injunction fits with earlier words, "Do not store up for yourselves treasures on earth . . . but store up for yourselves treasures in heaven. . . . For where your treasure is, there your heart will be also" (Matthew 6:19–21). To give oneself to the earthly is idolatry because this is to worship the temporary creation rather than the eternal Creator. Money itself is not evil, but the "love of money" is (1 Timothy 6:10)! Only God is worthy of our worship.

Jesus' command not to worry about our life (i.e., mortal existence) and about what we eat and drink and wear (Matthew 6:25) does not mean that these are not essential. Jesus himself fed hungry people (14:15–21), and the final judgment has to do with food and drink and clothing (25:35–36; note also God's meeting hunger and thirst in the Isaiah reading, 49:9–10).

What it does mean is that mortal life (*psyche*, Matthew 6:25), with its rightful concern for food and drink, cannot be our first focus, nor can our body (*soma*, 6:25) with its rightful concern for clothing. Life that centers on food, drink, and clothing is another form of idolatry that worships the created rather than the Creator.

Jesus, as he often does in his parables, turns to examples from God's creation to make his point: birds, lilies and grass. If God feeds the worry-free birds, why not trust in the God who values human beings most of all (6:26)? Worrying accomplishes nothing (6:27); trust is everything (the reading from 1 Corinthians also speaks of trust, 4:1–2).

If God clothes the worry-free lilies with the greatest of beauty and clothes the grass, alive today and gone tomorrow, why not trust God for clothing, "you of little faith" (6:28–30; note Matthew's use of "little faith" also in 8:26; 14:31; 16:8)?

It is people of "little faith" who worry about food, drink, and clothing (6:31–32; Matthew's Jewish-Christian readers would understand "Gentiles" or "nations" as unbelievers in the God of Israel). God knows the need for these necessities of life, but they are never to be the primary focus for people of faith.

No, "strive first for the [dominion] of God and [God's] righteousness, and all these things will be given to you as well" (6:33). God's reign of what is just and right was the center of Jesus' ministry, and it is the center of life for his faithful followers (note also 5:6: "Blessed are those who hunger and thirst for righteousness, for they will be filled"). The true and faithful food and drink is the higher righteousness which Jesus' ministry unfolds: "justice and mercy and faith" (23:23). This is what Matthew wanted for his readers.

"So do not worry about tomorrow, for tomorrow will bring worries of its own. Today's trouble is enough for today" (6:34). In our contemporary world, who would argue with that statement? But the way to meet the troubles of life is with a deep sense of trust in the God who cares about birds and lilies and grass, and us!

Respond to the Word

- How can you support others who may not have learned how to trust God?
- What step(s) will you take this week to seek God's dominion first in your life?

Go with the Word

Suzanne Marshall, *Journey Through Time*, Clayton, Missouri.
Photograph by RED ELF. Used by permission.

If you do not observe Transfiguration Sunday, use the session for
Proper 4 (page 190) next week.

We Were Witnesses

For we did not follow cleverly devised myths when we made known to you the power and coming of our Lord Jesus, but we had been eyewitnesses of Jesus' majesty. For Jesus received honor and glory from God when that voice was conveyed by the Majestic Glory, saying, "This is my child, my Beloved, with whom I am well pleased." We ourselves heard this voice come from heaven, while we were with Jesus on the holy mountain.

2 Peter 1:16–18

Bible Reading: 2 Peter 1:16–21

Additional Bible Readings: Exodus 24:12–18/Psalm 2
or Psalm 99
Matthew 17:1–9

Enter the Word

- How do eyewitness accounts create credibility for events?
- What experiences of God's glory can you bear witness to?

Remember some family stories that relatives passed on to you. Think of the events retold, the persons involved, and the details included. Ponder how these stories form and give identity to your family. Think about the questions these stories may answer for a generation that never experienced the recounted events.

Now consider the church's first generation, that is, those who had direct experience of Jesus' life and teaching. Read the story of the Transfiguration in Matthew 17:1–9. Envision yourself on the mountain with Peter, James, and John as you read. Experience the emotions that might have welled up within you. Think about how Jesus' transfiguration connects with experiences of transformation in your own life.

Imagine that fifty or more years have gone by. The generation of eyewitnesses to Jesus' ministry has dwindled. Imagine yourself as one of the few remaining eyewitnesses. Hear the questions that persons new to the faith are asking you, as well as ones raised by those who oppose Christianity. Rehearse what you might say to address the concerns of both the faithful and the opponents.

Read 2 Peter 1:16–21. Notice how the author asserts the credibility of this experience through a repeated series of "we were there" assertions. "We had been eyewitnesses" (1:16), "we ourselves heard" (1:18), and "we were with [Jesus]" (1:18). Notice too how the author abruptly shifts from "we" to "you" in verses 19b and 20. A new generation of faith must witness if the glory of Christ is to continue to claim and transform humanity.

Read the additional passages from Exodus and Psalms and draw connections between them and the Transfiguration story.

> *Praise to you, O God, for in the Transfiguration of Jesus*
> *I glimpse your power to transform me. Amen.*

Engage the Word

- What concerns does the author of 2 Peter address?

The author of 2 Peter calls himself "Simeon Peter, a servant and apostle of Jesus Christ" (2 Peter 1:1) and states that he was present at the Transfiguration of Jesus (1:18). Most modern scholars agree that the letter is probably "pseudonymous." In antiquity, pseudonymous writing (where one person writes in the name of another) was an accepted literary convention.

The author of 2 Peter, writing late in the first century, seeks to address two pressing issues for his readers: (1) the introduction of cleverly devised myths that contradict sound teaching (1:16); and (2) the delay of the Parousia, Jesus' coming (2 Peter 3). The two concerns are decisively interrelated.

The polemical tone of the writer of 2 Peter is unmistakable as he refutes false teaching. The delay of the Parousia has prompted scoffers to ridicule the believers' confidence in Christ's coming with such sentiments as: "Where is the promise of his coming?" (3:4). But the author exhorts his Christian readers to hope, for Christ will surely return. What appears to be a "delay" is actually an example of God's patient love, for God wants "all to come to repentance" (3:9).

If the delay of the Parousia has prompted scoffers to doubt, it has also provided an opportunity for false prophets to peddle their destructive and deceptive opinions. But the false teachers are heading for destruction (2:1–3).

In 2 Peter 1:16–21, the author shows that Jesus' Transfiguration, which revealed the majesty and power of God's Beloved Child, was seen and later preached by credible witnesses who had observed Jesus' life and had received his teachings. The Greek word for "eyewitnesses" in 1:16, *epoptai*, refers to those who have intimate knowledge of experiences or events. The writer certifies that the apostolic tradition is reliable.

The writer of Matthew narrates the Transfiguration account in Matthew 17:1–9. The "high mountain" is a place of revelation. Explicit in both the Matthean tradition and that of Mark and Luke (Mark 9:2–8; Luke 9:28–36) is that the disciples Peter, James, and John were eyewitnesses to the confirmation of the glory of God's Child. These three persons, who had witnessed the glory of Christ, had themselves experienced a marvelous transformation in their own lives, as Christian tradition shows.

The Transfiguration account recalls another scripture passage, Exodus 24:12–18, the story of Moses' ascent to Mount Sinai to receive the "tablets of stone, with the law and the commandment" (24:12). Mountains in the Judaeo-Christian tradition are often places of revelation of God's divine purposes for humankind.

Respond to the Word

- What witness can you make about your experience with God?
- What areas of your life will you open to God's transforming power this week?

Go with the Word

Christ, our Redeemer and Savior,
fill our hearts with love so that
we are forever transformed.
Claim our lives so that we may live
in perfect harmony with all living things.
Keep us focused on a life of service,
commitment, and Christian love.
Amen.

The Inviting Word Older Youth Learner's Guide (Cleveland, Ohio: United Church Press, 1995), 58. Used by permission.

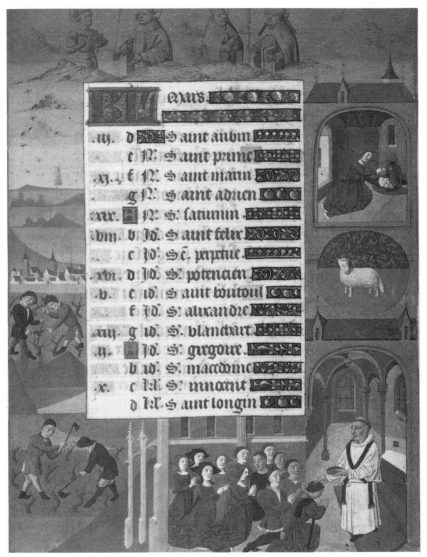

Manuscript illumination, *Receiving Ashes* (*March: Care of the Vines, Ash Wednesday*), from *The Hours of the Duchess of Bourgogne*, ca. 1450, Ms. 76/1362 fol. 3r., Musée Condé, Chantilly, France (Giraudon/Art Resource, N.Y.). Used by permission.

Lent

The celebratory mood of Epiphany gives way to the somber penitence of Lent. Ashes are symbolically placed on the foreheads of the contrite as a reminder that they have come from dust and will one day return to dust. Thus begins the spiritual journey that continues for forty days from Ash Wednesday through the night before Easter. The members of the community of faith, both corporately and individually, look inward and reflect on their readiness to follow Jesus as he journeys toward the cross. Most of this time of preparation is symbolized by purple, though the season is bracketed by the mourning black of Ash Wednesday and Good Friday. On Psalm/Passion Sunday red adorns the altar as a sign of the rejoicing throngs who greeted Jesus.

Look at the detail from an illuminated manuscript showing the faithful as ashes are imposed. Perhaps this ritual is familiar to you. Or maybe it has not been part of your religious tradition. Imagine yourself among those who are kneeling in prayer to receive the ashes. Ponder David's words: "Create in me a clean heart, O God, and put a new and right spirit within me. Cast me not away from your presence, and take not your holy spirit from me. Restore to me the joy of your salvation, and sustain in me a willing spirit" (Psalm 51:10–12). During this season of spiritual preparation, ask God to help you examine your own heart and restore you to wholeness and steadfast faithfulness.

Tempted

God said, "You shall not eat of the fruit of the tree that is in the middle of the garden, nor shall you touch it, or you shall die." But the serpent said to the woman, "You will not die; for God knows that when you eat of it your eyes will be opened, and you will be like God, knowing good and evil."

Genesis 3:3–5

Bible Reading: Genesis 2:15–17, 3:1–7

Additional Bible Readings: Psalm 32
                                 Romans 5:12–19
                                 Matthew 4:1–11

Enter the Word

- What temptations exist in today's society?
- What temptations ensnare you personally?

As you read Genesis 2:15–17 and 3:1–7, ponder its rich symbolism. This story has helped believers across the centuries understand how humanity fell out of favor with God by defying God's will. God asked for total devotion. God still asks for it. Yet God gave the man and the woman freedom of choice.

A serpent approached the woman in the garden and told her that the forbidden fruit was denied to them not because it might harm them but because God feared that she and her husband might become god-like after eating it. What a temptation! Power and knowledge were so close at hand. Imagine what the woman hoped to gain with that power or knowledge. Consider what people, including yourself, believe they can gain from god-like control and insight. Think specifically about what you long to grasp.

All of us are tempted in various ways. We sin. As Carl Jung says, "All the old primitive sins are not dead, but are crouching in the . . . corners of our modern hearts."[1] Peer into the corners of your heart and see what crouches there.

Paul explains in Romans 5:12–19 that the early temptation and sin of the first humans set the stage for the forgiveness that was to follow through Jesus Christ. As Lent begins we are reminded that the new covenant with the people is through Jesus. From the first temptation in the garden and the moment of sin, humanity floundered. God recognized the frailty of humanity and sent Jesus so that we could know God's grace.

> *Merciful God, cleanse my heart of willful striving and*
> *forgive my shortcomings and sins. Amen.*

Engage the Word

- How might this early story from Genesis have helped people confront their disobedience to God?

Genesis 2:4b–3:24 may belong to the earliest writing in Israel's history—that of the Yahwist (the writer used the Hebrew name Yahweh for God) who wrote in the tenth century before Jesus. Consider reading the entire section for the context of Genesis 2:15–17, 3:1–7. (Genesis 1:1–2:4a comes from the priestly writer some five hundred years later.)

For readers about the time of King David, the Yahwist wrote a poetic story to interpret some of the circumstances of human life: its creation, its temptation, its distortion of sexuality, its work, and the harmonious relationships God intended.

When Hebrew writers such as the Yahwist wanted to make a point, they did not speak abstractly about creation and sin. Rather, they often told stories to bear the message, sometimes using inclusive names (Eve means "life" and Adam means "humanity") to make their readers part of the story.

In Genesis 2:15–17, 3:1–7, God entrusted humanity to care for the garden. They were free to eat of every tree but one. God also gave to humans the gift of freedom (they are not puppets), but that freedom is neither to displace the Creator as the center of life nor to seize the power to determine good and evil for themselves. To make the creature the moral center leads to death (2:15–17). In Romans, Paul put it this way, "they exchanged the truth about God for a lie and worshiped and served the creature rather than the Creator" (Romans 1:25).

As the story unfolds in Genesis 3:1–7, the temptation to challenge the limits God puts on human freedom comes from the serpent. The evil that challenges God does not come from beyond the created world but from crafty forces within it who put the creature before the Creator and want to take God's place (3:5).

Further, the forbidden fruit can be very seductive: it appears to be "good," "a delight to the eyes"; it promises "to make one wise" (3:6). In the gospel reading for today, the devil promised Jesus all the dominions and glory of the world if only he would fall down and worship him. Jesus responded to this temptation by quoting from Deuteronomy, "Worship the Sovereign your God, and serve only God" (Matthew 4:10).

In the Genesis story, disobedience did not lead to promised delight but to painful distortion of human relationships and of human sexuality. Before disobedience, "the man and his wife were both naked, and were not ashamed" (2:25). After disobedience, "they knew that they were naked; and they sewed fig leaves together and made loincloths for themselves" (3:7). Innocence was lost.

Yet in the story, God still cares for them. Before they must leave the garden of Eden, "God made garments of skins for the man and his wife, and clothed them" (3:21).

In Romans, Paul contrasted the sinful disobedience of Adam with the graceful obedience of Christ; and "where sin increased, grace abounded all the more" (5:20). We are to obey God.

Respond to the Word

- How can you help others overcome their temptations?
- In what ways will you be more obedient to God this week?

Go with the Word

Si Fui Motivo de Dolor, Oh Dios
(If I Have Been the Source of Pain, O God)

Si fui motivo de dolor, oh Dios;
si por me causa el débil tropezó;
si en tus caminos yo no quise andar,
¡perdón, oh Dios!

Si vana y fútil mi palabra fue;
Si al que sufría en su dolor dejé;
no me condenes, tú, por mi maldad,
¡perdón, oh Dios!

Si por la vi da quise andar en paz,
tranquilo, libre y sin luchar por ti
cuando anhelabas verme en la lid,
¡perdón, oh Dios!

Escucha oh Dios, mi humilde confesión
u líbrame de tantación sutil;
preserva siempre mi alma en tu redil.
Amén, Amén.

If I have been the source of pain, O God;
If to the weak I have refused my strength;
If, in rebellion, I have strayed away;
Forgive me, God.

If I have spoken words of cruelty;
If I have left some suffering unrelieved;
Condemn not my insensitivity;
Forgive me, God.

If I've insisted on a peaceful life,
Far from the struggles that the gospel brings,
When you prefer to guide me into strife,
Forgive me, God.

Receive, O God, this ardent word of prayer,
And free me from temptation's subtle snare,
With tender patience, lead me to you care.
Amen, Amen.

Sara M. deHall, based on a text by C. M. Battersby, trans. Janet W. May, in *The New Century Hymnal* (Cleveland, Ohio: The Pilgrim Press, 1995), 544. English translation Copyright © 1992 by The Pilgrim Press. Used by permission.

Born   from   Above

Now there was a Pharisee named Nicodemus, a leader

of the Jews. He came to Jesus by night and said, "Rabbi,

we know that you are a teacher who has come from

God; for no one can do these signs that you do apart

from the presence of God." Jesus answered him, "Very

truly, I tell you, no one can see the dominion of God

without being born from above."

John 3:1–3

Bible Reading: John 3:1–17

Additional Bible Readings: Genesis 12:1–4a/Psalm 121
                                                        Romans 4:1–4, 13–17
                                                        Matthew 17:1–9

Enter the Word

- What do the words "born from above" (or "again") mean to you?
- If you believe you have been born from above, how would you describe this experience?

Read the story of Jesus and Nicodemus in John 3:1–17. This birth that Jesus speaks of does not happen only once, at the occasion of our physical birth. Nor does it happen just once, later in life. Rather, we are born from above again and again when we feel and remember the waters of baptism and when we experience the presence of the Spirit in our lives.

If possible, take a walk outside during the week. Weather permitting, try to spend some time outside on a sunny day and experience being bathed in God's sunlight. Close your eyes and concentrate on your feelings. If time outside in the sun isn't possible for you this week, take a few minutes to meditate and remember such an experience.

Consider the sun as an image of the new life God gives. Think about the ways in which you have experienced new life. Consider the possibilities that the assurance "born from above" opens up in your life. Identify areas of your life that yearn for new life.

Read the additional scriptures and consider how they might connect to the theme of new life given by God.

> *Open my heart and mind, O God, that I might receive*
> *new life from you. Amen.*

Engage the Word

- How would the story of Nicodemus' encounter with Jesus have helped John's community grow in their own faith?

The author of John states the major purpose for writing this Gospel: "so that you may come to believe that Jesus is the Messiah, the Child of God, and that through believing you may have life in his name" (John 20:31). From beginning to end, this gospel lifts Jesus in stories and symbols and words to strongly support belief in him as God's life-bringing Messiah. Why is this so? When John was written (toward the end of the first century), there were those who denied that Jesus was the Messiah. Persons were banned from the synagogue if they so believed in him (9:22, 34; 12:42; 16:2). The writer of John also had to challenge those who viewed John the Baptist as the Messiah (1:19–21; 3:28). Note how the writer's community enters into the testimony with the "we" of John 3:11.

The story of Nicodemus points to a synagogue leader who came secretly by night to investigate Jesus. He had seen God at work in Jesus' words and deeds. Given this gospel's often strong symbolic overtones, "by night" also may reflect Nicodemus' own personal desire for new light in his life (note that later he defends Jesus in 7:50–51 and buries him in 19:39–40).

Yet nowhere does John say that Nicodemus became a believer in Jesus. Does he represent those secret believers who feared to confess Jesus openly lest they be banned from the synagogues?

In the story, Nicodemus misunderstood Jesus' words about being born. The misunderstanding hinged on the double meaning of the Greek word *anothen*. It can mean either "again" or "from above." Nicodemus understood it as the former, but Jesus intended the latter. Thus "born again" is not the phrase for birth as believers in Jesus; "born from above" is. All Christians are "born from above"; that is, all have new life from the gift of God's dominion, God's reign of love in Jesus Christ that gave of itself all the way to death on a cross.

What does it mean to be born of water and the Spirit? Only John's Gospel tells of the piercing of Jesus' side with the outpouring of blood and water (19:34). Blood points to the outpouring of God's love in Jesus' death, water to the new life that flows from that love. God's Spirit makes that historic event of the cross in the past available to believers in the present. Christians are born as the Spirit makes the flowing water of God's love in Jesus present for them and as they respond to that love.

Human beings cannot manipulate or control that Spirit (3:8). God breathes and blows (spirit, breath, and wind all translate the one Greek word *pneuma*). God's love is a gift (3:16), made present by the Spirit to bring life to all who receive it.

In the Hebrew Scriptures Moses lifted up the serpent to bring healing. Similarly, Jesus, who descended from above, is lifted up on the cross as the Ruler, Judge, and one who brings God's new world and God's healing, non-condemning, saving love. That love gives eternal life, not only as life beyond death but as a new quality of life now.

Respond to the Word

- What would you say to a person like Nicodemus who is searching for new life?
- What questions will you ask Jesus as you encounter him in prayer this week?

Go with the Word

"Who are you?" she exclaimed, as the vision brightened into a form distinct, beaming with the beauty of holiness, and radiant with love. She then said, audibly addressing the mysterious visitant—"I *know* you, and I *don't* know you." Meaning, "You seem perfectly familiar; I feel that you not only love me, but that you always *have* loved me—yet I know you not—I cannot call you by name." When she said, "I know you," the subject of the vision remained distinct and quiet. When she said, "I don't know you," it moved restlessly about, like agitated waters. So while she repeated, without intermission, "I know you, I know you," that the vision might remain—"Who are you?" was the cry of her heart, and her whole soul was in one deep prayer that this heavenly personage might be revealed to her, and remain with her. At length, after bending both soul and body with the intensity of this desire, till breath and strength seemed failing, and she could maintain her position no longer, an answer came to her, saying distinctly, "It is Jesus." "Yes," she responded, "it is *Jesus*."

Sojourner Truth, *Narrative of Sojourner Truth* (New York: Arno Press, 1878; New York Times, 1969), 67.

Living Water

A Samaritan woman came to draw water, and Jesus said to her, "Give me a drink." (The disciples had gone to the city to buy food.) The Samaritan woman said to Jesus, "How is it that you, a Jew, ask a drink of me, a woman of Samaria?" (Jews do not share things in common with Samaritans.) Jesus answered her, "If you knew the gift of God, and who it is that is saying to you, 'Give me a drink,' you would have asked that one, who would then have given you living water."

John 4:7–10

Bible Reading: John 4:5–42

Additional Bible Readings: Exodus 17:1–7/Psalm 95
                                 Romans 5:1–11

Enter the Word

- What qualities make water refreshing to drink?
- How is Jesus the source of living water in your life?

In the reading from John 4:5–42, water is a symbol for eternal life. During the week, be aware of the ways in which you use and enjoy water. Be conscious of the water in your life. Perhaps you feel invigorated by a morning shower or soothed by an evening bath. Be aware of how you feel when you drink water. Recognize water's importance in cooking and cleaning. Imagine a week without water or with a limited supply of water.

Water symbolically communicates that spirituality is as ordinary—yet as important—as water. Therefore, the spiritual life should be as much a part of everyday life as water is.

Water as a symbol of new life is incorporated into the life of the church as the ritual of baptism. Remember your baptism, if possible, and consider the symbolic role of water in baptism.

Christ is the source of living water. Identify the ways your life is connected to that source. List the areas of your life that need the living water of Christ to flow through them.

Also read about how God provided water in the desert for the parched Israelites (Exodus 17:1–7 and Psalm 95) and the life-saving work of Jesus on the cross (Romans 5:1–11).

> *Fill my cup, O Christ, with water drawn from the well of salvation. Amen.*

Engage the Word

• How does John's story help readers to better know Jesus?

In every story in John's Gospel, the central character is Jesus. The purpose is to proclaim him, his deeds, and his words. Secondary characters are also part of the stories. In the last week's reading (John 3:1–17) that character was Nicodemus, a teacher in Israel and a respected male member of the religious community. Though he came to question Jesus, there is nothing in the story that declares he ever confessed him as the Messiah.

In today's word in John, the secondary character is a Samaritan woman, one just the opposite of Nicodemus. From the perspective of the religious establishment, she was a foreigner, a person of mixed race, a religious heretic, and an immoral woman. But Jesus broke through the barriers of nation, race, religion, and gender to give this woman living water. She then knew him as the Messiah and became a missionary to her own people.

It is a powerful story of a breakthrough that transformed her life and the life of her people as they finally came to see Jesus as "truly the Savior of the world" (4:42). It makes specific the proclamation that "God so loved the *world*."

John's Gospel often employs contrasts. In the Nicodemus story, being "born again" physically contrasts with being born "from above." In the story of the Samaritan woman, the physical water of Jacob's well contrasts with Jesus' gift of God's living water.

For the writer of John and his community toward the end of the first century that living water was the water of God's love that flowed from the cross (see John 19:34), "a spring of water gushing up to eternal life" (4:14). Thus Jesus brings an abundant life that breaks and reaches beyond human barriers.

In today's story, Jesus uttered not one condemning word as he perceived the woman's past. The woman viewed Jesus as a prophet. He was a prophet who broke another barrier—the barrier between the worship places of Samaritans and Jews (4:21–22). God is spirit (4:24). Worship is not a matter of place but of the flowing spirit and truth of God's love (note Romans 5:5, 8).

Then came her words about the coming Messiah, and Jesus revealed to her (the first person to whom he does so in John) that he was the one (4:25–26). The words translated "I am he," *ego eimi*, are literally "I Am." John's readers would recall the God named "I am" in Israel (Exodus 3:14). This God was present and at work in Jesus.

Jesus' own disciples were surprised that Jesus as a Jewish man was talking with a despised Samaritan woman (John 4:27). But it was this talk that already had transformed her perception of Jesus and God's living water in him. She went to tell her own people and invited them to come and see (4:28–29).

In a world that subordinated women to men and sometimes silenced them (also in parts of the church in John's day), here a woman became a missionary with a message that transformed the life of her people. When the thirst-quenching, living water of God's love flows, it breaks human barriers.

Respond to the Word

- How can you use Jesus' living water to "irrigate" the lives of those who are spiritually parched?
- Where does living water need to spring up in your life? How will you allow that to happen?

Go with the Word

My Lord Is the Source of Love

My Lord is the source of Love; I, the river's course.
Let God's love flow through me. I will not obstruct it.
Irrigation ditches can water but a portion of the field;
the great Yangtze River can water a thousand acres.
Expand my heart, O Lord, that I may love yet more people.
The waters of love can water vast tracts,
nothing will be lost to me.
The greater the outward flow, the greater the returning tide.
If I am not linked to Love's source, I will dry up.
If I dam the waters of Love, they will stagnate.
Can I compare my heart with the boundless seas?
But abandon not the measure of my heart, O Lord.
Let the waves of your love still billow there!

Wang Weifan, in *Lilies of the Field*, trans. Janice and Philip Wickeri,
Foundation for Theological Studies in Southeast Asia, 1988, quoted in
Bread of Tomorrow: Prayers for the Church Year, ed. Janet Morley
(Maryknoll, N.Y.: Orbis Books, 1992), 136. Used by permission.

That We May Believe

Then the Pharisees also began to ask the man who had been blind how he had received his sight. He said to them, "Jesus put mud on my eyes. Then I washed, and now I see." Some of the Pharisees said, "This man is not from God, for he does not observe the sabbath." But others said, "How can a man who is a sinner perform such signs?" And they were divided. So they said again to the man who had been blind, "What do you say about Jesus? It was your eyes he opened."

John 9:15–17b

Bible Reading: John 9:1–41

Additional Bible Readings: 1 Samuel 16:1–13/Psalm 23
                                          Ephesians 5:8–14

Enter the Word

- What do your friends believe about Christ?
- What new vision of Christ do you need to "see" in your life?

Perhaps you have heard the saying "Seeing is believing." Yet, when photographs of the moon walk and the tearing down of the Berlin Wall first appeared, some people still could not believe that these things had happened. When photographs of German concentration camps and American relocation camps for Japanese Americans became public after World War II, there was disbelief that injustice at such a scale had occurred. Even eyewitnesses could not make people believe.

Such was the circumstance of the Pharisees who set about to investigate the case of the man who was born without sight and then made to see by Jesus. The evidence was before them. The proof was alive in the man himself. Yet the Pharisees, wary and skeptical, could not believe. Neither their senses nor their reasoning could comprehend what their hearts could not believe.

As we look at the Pharisees, we might easily recognize their lack of vision—and our own. Recall a time in your own life when your heart could not embrace and believe. Perhaps you were confronted with one of God's many miracles, but something stood in the way of your believing. Explore the barrier(s) to belief and how you have overcome it.

Imagine yourself as the person born without sight who is healed by Jesus. Try to feel the joy of that first moment when everything you previously had only touched or smelled was now revealed to your sight. Now, think of a moment when an insight or truth was revealed to you through your faith in Jesus Christ.

In addition to the passage from John 9, also read the beloved Psalm 23. Study the passages from 1 Samuel and Ephesians.

Open my eyes that I may see you clearly, O God. Amen.

Engage the Word

• What literal and figurative messages does John express?

John 9:1–41 is one of the most dramatic stories in John's Gospel. It involves Jesus, a sightless man, Jesus' disciples, the sightless man's neighbors and others who knew him, the Pharisees, and the sightless man's parents. In the unfolding dialogues, the man who is sightless "sees" more and more of who Jesus is and comes to believe in him. On the other hand, the religious leaders who *think* they "see" are "blinded" to the truth.

Like other deeds of Jesus in this gospel, the healing of the man is a sign that points to something about Jesus and calls for believing in him. Here it is, "I am the light of the world" (John 9:5; note also

8:12). Jesus' feeding of the multitude pointed to "I am the bread of life" (6:35), his raising of Lazarus to "I am the resurrection and the life" (11:25).

The physical healing of the man who is sightless was only the beginning. The "seeing" moved from physical sight to seeing Jesus as a person (9:11), a prophet (9:11), the Messiah (9:22), God's coming Ruler and Judge ("Son of Man," 9:35; see Daniel 7:13–14). Finally the man said, "Lord, I believe" (9:38). He moved from physical sightlessness to spiritual sight.

The movement was the opposite for the religious leaders. They moved from physical seeing to spiritual sightlessness (9:39–41). They failed to see Jesus as the light of the world and tried repeatedly to discredit both Jesus and the man's testimony. Yet again and again the man met his antagonists with conviction and a ringing defense of the one who had opened his eyes.

At the beginning of the story, Jesus challenged the view, held even by Jesus' disciples, that the man's condition was due to his or his parent's sin. Rather, that condition provided an opportunity to reveal God, the great I Am's healing work in Jesus as the light of the world (9:2–5). The religious leaders called both Jesus and the man sinners (9:16, 24, 34). They were the sinners because they claimed to see but rejected the light that brings sight (9:41).

The light theme was central to John's community (see 1:4–5, 9, 3:19–21, 8:12, 12:35–36; note also Ephesians 5:8–14). One text reads, "And this is the judgment [Greek: *krisis*], that the light has come into the world, and people loved darkness rather than the light" (John 3:19). Judgment in John is not that of condemnation (note 3:17) but the crisis of decision for or against the light in Jesus.

The story in John 9:1–41 involved John's community toward the end of the first century in a conflict with the synagogue. Some of them had been banned from the synagogue (see John 9:22, 34). They and the one in whom they saw the light of the world had been challenged as sinners. Like the man born without sight, they too could say, "One thing I do know, that though I was blind, now I see" (9:25).

Respond to the Word

- How can you offer sight to the spiritually blind?
- What spiritual blindness will you lift to God for healing?

Go with the Word

According to the Gospels, Jesus' miracles were real, specific, and discernible events. Yet they occurred in an atmosphere of eschatological expectation and faith. When wrenched from this context, they look like the works of a magician or sorcerer. In his own time and in the earliest church the question of miracle could not be separated from faith in Jesus' preaching and power, both of which had to do with the kingdom of God. Faith could not, and cannot prove the miracles happened; faith provides the context in which their meaning can be discussed.

Robert A. Spivey and D. Moody Smith, *Anatomy of the New Testament: A Guide to Its Structure and Meaning* (New York: Macmillan, 1982), 220.

Can These Bones Live?

The hand of God came upon me, and God brought me out by the spirit of God and set me down in the middle of a valley; it was full of bones. God led me all around them; there were very many lying in the valley, and they were very dry. God said to me, "Mortal, can these bones live? I will lay sinews on you, and will cause flesh to come upon you, and cover you with skin, and put breath in you, and you shall live; and you shall know that I am God."

Ezekiel 37:1–3b, 6

Bible Reading: Ezekiel 37:1–14

Additional Bible Readings: Psalm 130
                                                           Romans 8:6–11
                                                           John 11:1–45

Enter the Word

- What needs to be rejuvenated in your life, church, and community?
- How does God give you life and hope?

Be alert this week for images of new life. Look at the natural world for melting snow, plants pushing up through soil, flowers bursting into bloom. Look within yourself for stirrings of hope, laughter, healing. Look at life in your community for examples of kind deeds, programs, or projects that alleviate human need and bring hope for new life.

Set aside some time and find a quiet comfortable place where you will not be disturbed. Read Ezekiel 37:1–14 out loud. Identify the images the writer uses to convey his message. Decide which of these images is the most meaningful to you. Recall times when you may have you felt like a pile of dry bones—lifeless and lacking purpose. Remember when you have felt exiled—cut off from what is most meaningful to you. Ponder the prophet's role in the story. Discern how God is bringing new life to you and to the life of your community.

As you read the additional passages from Psalm 130, Romans 8:6–11, and John 11:1–45, be alert for words of hope and renewal that may bring new life to your own spirit.

> *Breathe on me, O God, that I might be enlivened by your Spirit. Amen.*

Engage the Word

- Had you been among the exiles of Ezekiel's day, how would you have responded to his prophetic words?

Ezekiel was a prophet in the midst of the Exile in Babylon. Jerusalem with its Temple had been destroyed and many of the people of Israel carried away into captivity and exile in the years 597 and 587 before Jesus' coming.

The life of Israel had been devastated, and it was both a national disaster and a crisis of their faith in God. With the Temple as God's dwelling place destroyed and with their ruler also a captive (see 2 Kings 25:27–30), it is not surprising that they asked if the history of God with them had ended.

It was in this context that Ezekiel, led by God's Spirit, had the prophetic vision of a valley full of dry bones. Ezekiel 37:1–10 tell of the vision, and verses 11–14 interpret it. Typical of such prophetic visions, there is a dialogue between God and the prophet. God speaks first, "Mortal, can these bones live?" (37:3).

Knowing that he does not have the answer and that God is the only source of life, Ezekiel responded, "O Sovereign, you know."

But then God called for Ezekiel's participation as a prophet in prophesying to the bones: "O dry bones, hear the word of God," and in that word God promises breath (or "spirit," the Hebrew can be translated as either; see also Genesis 2:7) and new life. Ezekiel responded to God's command to prophesy and it happened: bones and breath enliven a vast multitude.

God then interpreted the bones as the "whole house of Israel" (Ezekiel 37:11). They complained, "Our bones are dried up, and our hope is lost; we are cut off completely" (37:11). But God promised life from such a critical situation and a return to the land of Israel. The exiles as a people shall know God's life-giving spirit back on their own soil. When that happens, they will know that God has indeed spoken and acted as the bones live again. It did happen. God's word to the prophet could be trusted.

This "resurrection" was long before Jesus' resurrection and pointed to God's power to bring new life in the midst of human existence now in this world. Though Jesus' resurrection does promise victory over death, it also promises new life now. In the gospel reading for today, Martha affirmed her Jewish belief in the future resurrection of the dead, but Jesus said to her, "I am the resurrection and the life" (John 11:25). God's love for the world not only brings new life beyond death; it brings new life now.

Just as Ezekiel emphasizes the power of God's breath or spirit to give new life, the Epistle reading for today also is strong on the work of the Spirit: "For the law of the Spirit of life in Christ Jesus has set you free from the law of sin and of death. . . . To set the mind on the flesh [creaturely] is death, but to set the mind on the things of the Spirit is life and peace . . . life to your mortal bodies" (Romans 8:2, 6, 11).

Psalm 130, like the passage from Ezekiel, expresses a cry of despair. But the psalm also testifies to hope in the steadfast love and the redeeming power of God to give life to dry bones.

Respond to the Word

- How can you, working with others, breathe new life into an individual, community, or organization?
- Where in your own life do you need to see signs of hope and renewal? What steps will you take toward renewal this week?

Go with the Word

A Sign of Hope in a Valley of Dry Bones

Chronically plagued by drought, disease, and devastating poverty, Haiti is the poorest country in this hemisphere. Seeing the people and animals, skin-and-bone hungry and dehydrated, I remarked to one of the others on our mission trip there, "This is a valley of dry bones."

Yet that same day, in a small hospital for children in Port au Prince, the cheerful director, Gladys Sylvestre, was encouraging a tiny girl named Jeanette as she was taking her very first steps—at age three and a half. The child's sandals were scuffed hand-me-downs, as was her dress. Much of her hair had fallen out, from malnutrition. Yet her enormous brown eyes were bright as she beamed up at us, thrilled with the adventure and accomplishment of learning to walk.

Gladys told us she had discovered Jeanette several months before, abandoned as hopelessly ill and left to die in the city's General Hospital. "Something about her just made me stop and notice. She called out for me to help her, and I just couldn't leave her there." So Gladys arranged for the little girl to come home with her, and in the weeks to follow, Jeanette underwent surgery and rehabilitation. The day we met she was vibrant, holding onto Gladys' hand and taking wobbly but determined steps on fragile bones across the nursery floor.

Enjoying our smiles and applause for her achievement, she began swaying, bobbing her head back and forth, all the while grinning at us to beat the band! Gladys laughed and spoke in Creole to Jeanette, who answered, "M'ap danse ak bondye!"

I said, "Would you translate?"

Jeanette's rescuer smiled, "I asked her, 'Jeanette, are you dancing?' She said, 'I'm dancing with God!'"

In the valley, dry bones lived again.

Deborah Grant Rose, in *The Inviting Word Older Youth Learner's Guide* (Cleveland: United Church Press, 1995), 68. Used by permission.

Blessed Is the One

When they had come near Jerusalem and had reached Bethphage at the Mount of Olives, Jesus sent two disciples, saying to them, "Go into the village ahead of you, and immediately you will find a donkey tied, and a colt with it; untie them and bring them to me." The crowds that went ahead of Jesus and that followed were shouting, "Hosanna to the Son of David! Blessed is the one who comes in the name of God! Hosanna in the highest heaven!"

Matthew 21:1–2, 9

Bible Reading: Matthew 21:1–11

Additional Bible Readings: Psalm 118:1–2, 19–29
Isaiah 50:4–9a/Psalm 31:9–16
Philippians 2:5–11
Matthew 26:14–27:66
or Matthew 27:11–54

Enter the Word

- Why might the crowd have called Jesus "blessed"?
- Had you been in the crowd at Jerusalem when Jesus entered, what words might you have shouted as he passed?

Imagine that a filmmaker created a movie based on the Gospel of Matthew. Jesus' triumphal entry into Jerusalem (Matthew

21:1–11) might feature happy, boisterous music, typical of a parade. But there would also be another musical theme, one with ominous tones, playing under the parade theme. Such a soundtrack would faithfully portray the mood and action of this passage.

As the film begins to roll in your mind, watch for the contrasts between Jesus the humble man and Jesus the sovereign ruler. Try to imagine the details of scenery that a filmmaker might focus on, as well as ways to depict Jesus as both servant and sovereign.

Think about when you need Jesus to be the ruler of all life and when you need him to be a humble servant. Keep in mind that both perceptions are correct. He is not a one-dimensional savior. Jesus, our supreme example of humanity, demonstrates that there are some situations when you need to be an authority figure and others when you need to be in the background. Ponder situations in your life where you need to be the servant or an authority figure.

Read the additional passages and notice links in these scriptures that may connect them to the humble sovereign, Jesus.

> *I sing and shout Hosanna to you, O Blessed One, for you are the humble servant and savior of all. Amen.*

Engage the Word

- How did Matthew's account help readers experience the rejoicing and suffering of Palm/Passion Sunday?

Joining Passion Sunday and Palm Sunday calls for combining aspects of both rejoicing and suffering. Jesus rode into Jerusalem with shouts of "Hosanna in the highest heaven" (Matthew 21:9), but days later he went on to die with shouts of "Let him be crucified" (27:22–23). There can be no movement from Palm Sunday to Easter Sunday without going through Good Friday.

The Christ hymn in the Epistle reading from Philippians presents this movement from Christ's emptying and humbling himself, to his death, to his exaltation. The confession of Jesus to the glory of God at the end of the hymn does not bypass "obedient to the point of death—even death on a cross" (Philippians 2:8; note also the Isaiah and Psalm 31 readings).

The writer of Matthew was an early Christian teacher toward the end of the first century. Jesus' words in Matthew 13:52 show something of Matthew's own self-understanding as one who joined together what is old in his Hebrew heritage and what is new in Jesus Christ and the early church.

His gospel is organized in blocks as a kind of manual for instructing early Christians, many of whom were persons of Jewish heritage who needed to see how Jesus connected to them and fulfilled their scriptures. He does this in Matthew 21:1–11 by relating Jesus to Isaiah 62:11, Zechariah 9:9, and Psalm 118:25–26.

Matthew used and largely followed Mark's Gospel. Unlike Mark, Matthew quoted from the prophet Zechariah to present Jesus as fulfilling that scripture as he rode into Jerusalem (Matthew 21:4–5). Because of how he interpreted Zechariah, Matthew depicts Jesus as riding into Jerusalem on two animals (21:7).

Jesus' entrance from the Mount of Olives gave it messianic overtones. But it is not the entrance of a crushing conqueror, though this may have been what the people hoped for. It was the entrance of a self-giving servant who rode on without compromise to save others, not to save himself (Matthew 27:42).

As "the whole city went wild with excitement" (NEB), the cry "Hosanna [O save] to the Son of David" had political and military overtones. They may have wanted a political Messiah of power. But the one whom they blessed was a prophetic Messiah of passion—of suffering and death and, finally, of resurrection.

Unlike Mark, what follows immediately in Matthew is Jesus' cleansing of the Temple. This humble king did not retreat from attacking those forces of corruption that made God's house of prayer a den of robbers. If there was one thing that Jesus could not stomach, it was the hypocrisy of religious leaders and their exploitation of others. His opposition to them played a major role in bringing about his passion and death.

As Jesus entered Jerusalem, he was not blessed because he was a conquering sovereign. He was blessed because he rode on to die as a self-giving servant who saved others.

Respond to the Word

- How can you invite others to be in Jesus' presence today?
- Envision yourself among the spectators shown on *Blessed Is He*. What commitment will you make to honor Jesus?

Go with the Word

José Faustino Altramirano, *Blessed Is He*, as reproduced in Philip and Sally Scharper, eds., *The Gospel in Art by the Peasants of Solentiname* (Maryknoll, N.Y.: Orbis Books). Used by permission of Verlagsleiter, Peter Hammer Verlag.

Bagong Kussudiardja (Indonesia), *The Ascension*, as reproduced in
Masao Takenaka and Ron O'Grady, *The Bible Through Asian Eyes*
(Auckland, New Zealand: Pace Publishing in association with the
Asian Christian Art Association, 1991), 165. Used by permission of
the Asian Christian Art Association.

Easter

Instead of finding a sealed tomb, the women who had come at dawn on Sunday are greeted by an angel who announces astonishing news: "Jesus has been raised from the dead" (Matthew 28:7). The heavenly messenger invites the mourners to inspect the empty tomb and then go and tell the disciples that the Crucified One is alive!

Baptisms and initiations into the church often occur during this festive Easter season that is sometimes known as the Great Fifty Days. The liturgical color for this season is white, calling for the new life that is offered by Christ the Risen Sovereign. When the season ends on Pentecost Sunday, the white paraments are replaced with red ones. These altar cloths remind the community of faith of the tongues of fire that God poured out upon the disciples. Barriers of language and culture were transcended on Pentecost as the disciples spoke in diverse languages to proclaim God's power and deeds to all persons.

Study the painting *The Ascension* by the Indonesian artist Bagong Kussudiardja. How does it reflect your own understanding of Christ's ascension into heaven? How would you portray this amazing event? What difference does Jesus' resurrection and ascension make in your own life? With whom will you share the wondrous news that Jesus is risen?

Go and Tell

The angel said, "Do not be afraid; I know that you are looking for Jesus who was crucified. Jesus is not here; but has been raised, as he said. Come, see the place where Jesus lay. Then go quickly and tell the disciples, 'Jesus has been raised from the dead, and indeed is going ahead of you to Galilee; there you will see Jesus.' This is my message for you."

Matthew 28:5b–7

Bible Reading: Matthew 28:1–10

Additional Bible Readings: Acts 10:34–43 or Jeremiah 31:1–6/
          Psalm 118:1–2, 14–24
          Colossians 3:1–4 or Acts 10:34–43
          John 20:1–18

Engage the Word

- What is the Easter message that is to be told?
- How does this message affect your life?

Read Matthew 28:1–10 several times, perhaps once aloud. As you read, be aware of the images that come to mind, such as the feel of an earthquake and the sight of the angel. Also pay attention to the emotion of the characters involved. Ponder how people can feel fear and joy at the same time, as in verse 8. Now experience your own emotions as you contemplate this amazing scene.

"Quickly" is a word that appears twice in this passage. Yet most Christians don't have a sense of urgency about the Easter message. Recall those times and places when you have been so excited by good news you couldn't wait to share it. Think about those "good news" experiences in your life and remember the way you felt in those moments. Now envision yourself going out quickly to tell the good news of Easter to others.

In the reading from Acts 10, Peter recognizes that he is to proclaim good news to all, without partiality. Jeremiah 31 also shows how all are included in God's loving care. Psalm 118 praises God for deliverance from enemies. Colossians gives hope to us because of Jesus' resurrection. John 20 recounts the first Easter.

> *Help me to go and tell the good news so that others might believe in the Resurrected One who came to save all humanity. Amen.*

Engage the Word

- How might Matthew's account of Easter have inspired his community to go and tell the news of Jesus' resurrection?

For all early Christian writers, Jesus' resurrection is the keystone in the arch of Jesus' life and ministry. Without God's raising Jesus from the dead to new life as the risen Christ, we never would have heard stories of his birth and ministry, his suffering and death. Christians are people of the resurrection.

But we need to distinguish the Easter stories from the Easter message. The Easter *stories* in each of the four gospels differ in details (e.g., compare Matthew with Mark 16:1–8), but each in its own way proclaims the same *message*: God has raised Jesus from death to life. Only the four gospels have stories of the empty tomb, but all early Christian writers believe in the message of Jesus' resurrection.

The differing details in the stories show that the gospel writers are not simple reporters. They each are shapers of stories that proclaim the risen Christ. They want their readers to believe in him and, like the women in Matthew's story, to "go and tell" that Jesus is alive.

There is a message in the details, too. A careful look at the details in Matthew's story reveal what he wanted to proclaim to his community some fifty years after Jesus' resurrection.

Matthew was a Christian teacher toward the end of the first century. He likely saw himself in Jesus' words in Matthew 13:52: a scribe (teacher), trained (discipled) for God's reign to bring out the old of his Hebrew heritage and join it with the new in Jesus as God's saving Messiah for both Jews and Gentiles.

Matthew wrote that the event occurred "after the sabbath [Saturday], as the first day of the week [Sunday] was dawning" (28:1). For Christians every Sunday is a celebration of God's raising Jesus from the dead to be alive forever.

Matthew's story spoke of an earthquake. For him, Jesus' resurrection is not only for human beings to tell but for nature to proclaim as well. He spoke of an angel, God's "messenger," who rolled away the stone from the door of the cave-tomb. Power over death is not a human power but God's. That power is superior to religious and political leaders and their cohorts (28:4; see also 27:64–66).

The angel's proclamation to the women is the heart of the story: "He is not here; for he has been raised" (28:6). They were not to fear but to go and tell Jesus' disciples that he is alive. They would see him in their home territory of Galilee, and they did (28:16–20).

In a setting that often made women subordinate to men, it is striking that women were the first to tell the story of Jesus' resurrection. In Matthew's story Jesus commissioned them twice to "go and tell" (28:7, 10). The risen Jesus met these joyous women on their way and greeted them. They took hold of him and worshiped him—the one in whom God was so powerfully at work and who had entrusted them with such a message.

The spiritual proclaims, "Go, tell it on the mountain, that Jesus Christ is born." Even more: Go, tell that he has been raised.

Respond to the Word

- How can your faith community reach out and tell others, in both word and deed, the good news of Jesus?
- To whom will you go and personally tell about Jesus this week?

Go with the Word

The Day of Resurrection

The day of resurrection! Earth, tell it out abroad;
the Passover of gladness, the Passover of God.
From death to life eternal, from earth unto the sky,
our Christ has brought us over with hymns of victory.

Our hearts be pure from evil, that we may see aright
the Christ who reigns eternal in resurrection light;
We listen for the teachings once heard so calm and plain,
for we, too, want to follow and raise the victor strain.

Now let the heavens be joyful, let earth its song begin,
the whole world keep high triumph, and all that is therein;
Let all things seen and unseen their notes of gladness blend,
for Christ again has risen, our joy that has no end.

John of Damascus, 8th century, trans. John Mason Neale, 1862, alt; in
The New Century Hymnal (Cleveland: The Pilgrim Press, 1995), 245.
Used by permission.

R o o m   f o r   D o u b t

Jesus said to Thomas, "Have you believed because you have seen me? Blessed are those who have not seen and yet have come to believe."

John 20:29

Bible Reading: John 20:19–31

Additional Bible Readings: Acts 2:14a, 22–32/Psalm 16
                                                    1 Peter 1:3–9

Engage the Word

- How have you seen people respond to those who have doubts about their faith?
- What doubts do you have about your own faith?

This week's lesson features a famous "doubter." Take a moment to jot down some of your own questions or doubts related to faith. Put a star by the ones that concern you most. Circle the ones you have learned to live with.

Read John 20:19–31. In many ways Thomas is the most modern of the disciples. Often today persons tend to be skeptical of things they cannot see. Moreover, they generally assume that what science cannot explain is not true. Perhaps you, or people you know, feel that way. The risen Christ seems to address this problem when he says, "Blessed are those who have not seen and yet have come to believe" (John 20:29).

Actually, the late first-century audience to whom the author wrote the gospel was in a similar position. A few early disciples were privileged to see and touch Jesus, but others had to experience the risen Christ in a different way. Verses 30 and 31 clearly state the gospel writer's reason for including this story: "Now Jesus did many other signs in the presence of his disciples, which are not written in this book. But these are written so that you may come to believe that Jesus is the Messiah, the Child of God, and that through believing you may have life in his name" (20:30–31).

Continue your study by reading the additional passages from Acts, Psalm 16, and 1 Peter.

> *I admit it, Gracious God. I'm a doubter. Help thou my unbelief. Amen.*

Enter the Word

- How could John's account of Jesus' resurrection appearances strengthen the beliefs of his own community of faith?

Three of the four gospels have stories of Jesus' appearance after God raised him from the dead (Mark does not), but they all differ from one another. Each author has shaped his own declaration of these appearances to meet the needs of the communities for whom they were written. By proclaiming these appearances, the gospel writers emphasize the continuity between the crucified Jesus and the risen Christ. It really is Jesus who is alive again, whom God has raised to a new form of life to be present with his followers.

John 20:19–31 records two appearances of the risen Jesus to his disciples. But another appearance precedes them, the one to Mary Magdalene (John 20:11–18). In that cultural setting, it is surprising that a woman, not the male disciples, first proclaimed the risen Christ (20:18). Jesus commissioned her to go and tell (20:17).

In John's story of Jesus' first appearance to the disciples, Jesus came to them in their fear behind locked doors. They had deserted him (16:32), but he did not desert them. He brought to them "peace," *shalom*—God's wholeness, health, and intact relationship with them—and their fear turned into joy. In John's story, Jesus' showing them his wounds proclaimed that he really was the crucified Jesus whom God raised from the dead and who now reestablished his relationship with them.

This first appearance to them became their "ordination" for ministry. Jesus' mission of God's love for the world (3:16) became their mission with God's Holy Spirit (or breath), just as God's breathing earlier had empowered humanity for life (Genesis 2:7). Jesus' task of taking away the sin of the world (John 1:29)—to take away the brokenness of relationship with God and the ensuing broken relationships with others—now became their task. That task continued for John's community some sixty years later.

Doubt about Jesus' resurrection was part of the experience of Jesus' first disciples. (Note also Matthew 28:17 and Luke 24:11). Thomas was not there at Jesus' first appearance. He doubted and would not believe the testimony of the others (John 20:24–25). But with his own experience of the risen Christ he made the moving confession, "My Lord and my God" (20:28). He saw that Israel's God had indeed raised Jesus to new life.

In John's story those first disciples saw the risen Christ. But John's own community did not have that experience. Therefore, Jesus' final words in the story of "doubting Thomas" spoke especially to them. "Blessed are those who have not seen and yet have come to believe" (20:29). These words speak also to believers today who have no tangible proof of the risen Christ. But he is alive for those who believe.

What finally is that belief? It is that Jesus is the Messiah, the Child of God, who gives life to those who believe (20:31). New life in Christ turns doubt into joyous affirmation.

Respond to the Word

- How can you be open to someone else's doubts while helping that person come to believe?
- How are you like Thomas? What steps will you take to face your own doubts and try to resolve them?

Go with the Word

The Younger Brother of Thomas

Thomas didn't really touch him.
I would have.
What can you prove just by looking?
Since when is seeing believing?
They killed my brother's friend
That's fact.
And Thomas just went crazy.
I was there.
It hurt to hear him cry like that.
I don't want to go crazy like Thomas has.
And then this story starts:
that Jesus isn't dead,
that he's been seen
walking through walls,
showing up at supper time.
But nobody, nobody had touched him.
Thomas didn't buy it.
I wouldn't have either.
Never listen to an eyewitness.
Get the facts firsthand.
Don't settle for someone
you can't get a hold of.
But then this ghost or hoax appeared
and called his name.
Thomas took one look
and thought that he'd seen God.
H really didn't touch him, see.
But doubting Thomas believes.
It would take more than that
to convince me.
Doubting runs in the family.

Heather Murray Elkins, "The Younger Brother of Thomas," *Accent on Youth* 7, no. 2 (spring 1985), 2. Used by permission.

Present at the Table

Then they told what had happened on the road, and how Jesus had been made known to them in the breaking of the bread.

Luke 24:35

Bible Reading: Luke 24:13–35

Additional Bible Readings: Acts 2:14a, 36–41/
    Psalm 116:1–4, 12–19
    1 Peter 1:17–23

Enter the Word

- Why are meals so important in the nurturing of relationships?
- When have you recognized the presence of Christ in your life?

Eavesdrop on the travelers who were discussing the death and resurrection of Jesus as you read Luke 24:13–35. According to the verses prior to this reading, they had heard the report of the women who had gone to the tomb; and they thought most people in the area must also know the story by now (24:1–11). Imagine their surprise when a stranger approached and asked them what they were talking about as if he had not heard.

They walk on, talking with the stranger, and they invite him to join them for the evening meal. Over supper their surprise turned to amazement, for as he broke and blessed the bread his identity was revealed. The risen Christ was with them.

Think for a moment about a recent gathering of friends, relatives, or the congregation where food was served. Someone proba-

bly said a blessing before the meal. Now imagine a stranger entering that group, talking with people, asking questions, laughing.
What if he stood up to give the blessing and those present immediately recognized him to be the risen Christ. Who would crowd
around him? What questions would be asked? Would some be too
awestruck to draw near or speak? How would you react?

When believers gather at the communion table, Christ is present. Notice how you recognize that presence as you participate in
the sacred meal. Read the poem entitled "Christ at the Table,"
found at the end of this chapter, for some ideas on ways that you
may encounter the risen Christ there. Think about how others
encounter the living Christ as they interact with you.

Acts 2 describes how the members of the early church focused
their attention on finding Christ as they joined with one another.
First Peter 1:17–23 also speaks about how believers are to live
together. In Psalm 116, the writer praises God for healing.

> *Open my eyes, my ears, and my heart that I may recog-*
> *nize the Beloved One wherever he is present. Amen.*

Engage the Word

- How might Luke's story have shaped his readers' faith?

Biblical writings witness repeatedly to the God who feeds people: Israel with manna in the wilderness; the widow and her son
through Elijah; the prophet Isaiah in exile; the multitudes in Jesus'
ministry; the disciples at the Last Supper; the disciples with the
risen Christ; the people from north, south, east, and west at the
heavenly messianic banquet.

Luke points to this feeding theme in Mary's song (Luke 1:53),
in the feeding of the five thousand (9:12–17), in inviting the poor
and persons who were disabled (14:12–14), in celebrating the
return of the lost (15:23–24), and in observing the Passover and
the Last Supper (22:14–20).

The gospel writer witnesses further to this feeding theme as the
risen Christ broke bread with two disciples at Emmaus (24:13–35;
note also Acts 2:42 and 46). As Jesus had fed people before his crucifixion, he continued to feed them after his resurrection.

The Emmaus road story is one of the richest in Luke's Gospel.

It points to Jesus' crucifixion and the disciples' dashed hope. It points to Jesus' ministry, death, and resurrection. It points to Israel's scriptures and their link to Jesus. It points to disciples with a message to tell. Luke wove it all in.

The table scene is the climax of the story. From the table, the disciples could look back; and from the table, they could move forward. On the road, the risen Christ had been their companion; but they did not recognize him. As they told Jesus what had happened, the story of Jesus' words and deeds, his death and resurrection was told, including the witness of the women.

Even when Jesus interpreted their scriptures (Moses and the prophets) about the Messiah, who first must suffer before being raised in glory, they did not recognize him. However, when they invited him to stay and he "took bread, blessed and broke it, and gave it to them" (Luke 24:30), they recognized him.

As they looked back to his presence with them on the road and to his interpreting of scripture, they said, "Were not our hearts burning within us" (24:32). For Luke, the interpretation of scripture is not only for the head but for the heart.

They could not capture their experience with the risen Christ. He vanished from their sight. Nor could they simply linger in worship at the table. They had to take to the road and travel to Jerusalem. They had to tell the story of their experience with the risen Christ "in the breaking of the bread" (24:35).

Toward the end of the first century, Luke wanted his community to know that as they gathered around the communion table, they too would experience the presence of the risen Christ. From that table, they could look back on their path and know that Christ was with them even if they did not recognize that presence. From that table, they could take to the road in their world and tell the story—Christ is with us on the road and meets us at the table.

Respond to the Word

- What can you do to make others aware of Christ's presence?
- How would you respond if you dined with Christ this week?

Go with the Word

Christct at the Table

> I have stood with the congregation,
> Sipped from the cup,
> Tasted the bread.
> I have prayed with the congregation,
> for Christ to enter
> and fill my soul.
> I have looked at the faces around me,
> plain folk and fancy,
> old folk and young.
> I have searched for the face of Jesus,
> asked when Christ
> would appear.
> Have I looked past the face of Jesus?
> Have I not seen the Christ in another?
> Have I missed him at the table?
> I will stand again with the congregation
> and look for Christ
> in their midst.

The Inviting Word Older Youth Learner's Guide (Cleveland, Ohio: United Church Press, 1995), 76. Used by permission.

Abundant Life

Day by day, as they spent much time together in the temple, they broke bread at home and ate their food with glad and generous hearts, praising God and having the good will of all people.

Acts 2:46–47a

Bible Reading: Acts 2:42–47

Additional Bible Readings: Psalm 23
1 Peter 2:19–25
John 10:1–10

Enter the Word

- How does society at large define "abundant life"?
- How would you describe "abundant life" as a Christian?

Take a few moments to consider some things you especially appreciate about life in your church community. List your ideas on paper. Jot down a few words to indicate why each item on your list is significant.

Now read Acts 2:42–47. Try to correlate this description of life in Christian community with your own experience. Consider how the two are similar and different. Try to discern reasons for these similarities and differences.

Aside from some clues in Paul's letters and some inferences scholars make from the Gospels, Luke's somewhat idealistic summary in Acts is our only information about those first-generation Christians. Thus, the passage is foundational to the church's understanding of the ideal life of a local congregation.

Think for a moment of the broad categories introduced here: the apostles' teaching, the breaking of bread, prayers, the support of friends, and the sharing of resources to meet one another's needs. Decide how well these broad categories describe the overall structure of your own congregation.

Perhaps when measured against the ideal, some shortcomings appear. Yet, we know from Paul's letters that some of the early Christian communities were far from conflict free. No church community will achieve perfection because the church is made up of human beings. But congregations can strive toward the ideal and help one another along the way with "glad and generous hearts" (Acts 2:46).

See how the additional passages may relate to the idea of abundant life.

> *Fill me with your abundant life, O God, that I may be a blessing to others. Amen.*

Engage the Word

• What are the signs of an abundant life community for Luke?
Acts 2:42–47 follows well last Sunday's reading from the Gospel of Luke. It moves from the first half of Luke's two-part work to the second; it also picks up the theme of "breaking bread" (Luke 24:30, 35; Acts 2:42, 46).

What happened before Pentecost with the two disciples at Emmaus continued in Luke's story of the early Christians after Pentecost. Luke wanted his community toward the end of the first century to know that what had nourished the ministry of the earliest Christians would also nourish theirs.

Luke wanted to underscore other aspects of the life of those earliest Christians. Acts 2:42–47 points to several aspects of the internal life of the community that were to nourish Christians for their external mission as witnesses to the ends of the earth (Acts 1:8).

One was the "apostles' teaching" (Acts 2:42). For Luke, the teaching of the twelve apostles was fundamental. They had been with Jesus in his ministry and were witnesses to Jesus' resurrection (note Luke's criteria for "apostle" in Acts 1:21–22). The apostles' teaching was rooted in their experience of both Jesus' ministry and his resurrection. For Luke, Christian education was essential.

Another aspect was the "fellowship," the *koinonia*, the partnership, the supportive community. The Christian mission was not for lone individuals. It was a communal task. They needed one another to meet the hard work that faced them in an often hostile world. Luke deeply appreciated the church as community.

For Luke, the worship of the community was central, both in the temple of the early Christians' Jewish roots and in their homes. The breaking of bread and the prayers were integral parts of their life. Being at table together with the risen Christ nourished them with his presence. Luke placed much emphasis on Jesus as a person of prayer, and the Christian community needed to follow Jesus in this empowering communication with God.

For Luke, these aspects in the life of the early Christians—teaching, support, Holy Communion, prayer—were essential. But there were also the deeds—the "wonders and signs" (Acts 2:43)—that continued Jesus' deeds of healing (for example, Acts 3:1–10).

Further, with Luke's strong concern for the poor and for the right use of this world's possessions, he pointed to the early Christians' sharing of their goods to meet economic needs. It was a kind of "communism" (2:44–45), not a coercive political system, but an expression of their generosity to reflect God's generosity toward them. Their life together praised God, created good will among the people, and added to their number those touched by God's healing, saving good news (2:47).

The words of today's theme come from Jesus' words in John's gospel: "I came that they may have life, and have it abundantly" (John 10:10). Luke's portrayal of the early community spells out some details of that life for his community and for ours.

Respond to the Word

- How can you help your congregation move toward Luke's ideal of an abundant life community?
- What personal changes do you need to make to be the kind of disciple Jesus intended members of the faith community to be?

Go with the Word

Luke presents us with an idealized moment in early Christian history. . . . We can learn much about life in the Christian community during the best of times. Notice that the life of faith was the passion of all the people remembered here. Indeed, faith focused the life of these people with one another, so that they gave themselves to what they had in common, not what distinguished them from one another. In this context, the members of the community accomplished great things that, in turn, brought a sense of awe to the whole community.

Marion Soards, Thomas Dozeman, and Kendall McCabe, *Year A, Lent/Easter: Preaching the Revised Common Lectionary* (Nashville: Abingdon, 1993), 136.

God's Own People

But you are a chosen race, a royal priesthood, a holy nation, God's own people, in order that you may proclaim the mighty acts of the one who called you out of the night into God's marvelous light. Once you were not a people, but now you are God's people; once you had not received mercy, but now you have received mercy.

1 Peter 2:9–10

Bible Reading: 1 Peter 2:2–10

Additional Bible Reading: Acts 7:55–60/
                                          Psalm 31:1–5, 15–16
                                          John 14:1–4

Enter the Word

- Who are God's people?
- Why do you consider yourself to be one of God's own people?

Take your Bible, pencil, and paper to a comfortable place and read the following quotation by Henri Nouwen.

> A life without a lonely place, that is, a life without a
> quiet center, easily becomes destructive. When we cling to
> the results of our actions as our only way of self-identifi-
> cation, then we become possessive and defensive and tend
> to look at our fellow human beings more as enemies to be
> kept at a distance than as friends with whom we share the

gifts of life. . . . In solitude we become aware that our
worth is not the same as our usefulness. . . . As a com-
munity of faith, we take the world seriously but never too
seriously. . . . As a community of faith we work hard,
but we are not destroyed by the lack of results. And as a
community of faith we remind one another constantly
that we form a fellowship of the weak, transparent to [the
One] who speaks to us in the lonely places of our exis-
tence and says: Do not be afraid, you are accepted.[1]

As you read 1 Peter 2:2–10 be aware that this scripture is about
God's own people. It was originally addressed to new Christians and
thus offers advice about growing in faith.

Ponder images that speak to you in terms of your own spiritual
growth. Try to apply some of the images or concepts to life in your
own congregation. Think about why this passages calls us to be "a
people" rather than a "person." Look for ways that Henri Nouwen's
comments help connect your need for solitude with your need for
community.

Also read the passages from Acts 7, Psalm 31, and John 14.

I give thanks, O God, for the holy people with whom I
am bonded in community. Amen.

Engage the Word

•   How would the writer of 1 Peter have helped his readers
    identify themselves as God's own people?

Like some of the New Testament letters written in Paul's name
(see "Engage the Word" for Proper 27), today's scripture from 1
Peter 2:2–10 is written in Peter's name. After his death in the sixties of the first century, others let Peter speak again to meet new
historical situations in the life of early Christians. This practice of
calling upon earlier authoritative persons was widespread in both
Jewish and Christian circles.

An interesting possibility is that a major part of 1 Peter incorporated a baptismal sermon (1 Peter 1:10–4:11) into the framework
of a letter. To read this scripture as a newly baptized person lets us
experience a kind of early preaching.

Some words in the initial verses fit well for new Christians: "newborn infants," "pure, spiritual milk," "grow into salvation," "tasted that the Lord is good" (1 Peter 2:2–3). These words point, not to people who have arrived, but to those who are at the beginning of their growth in the Christian life.

First Peter speaks of Jesus Christ as a stone, a living stone, rejected by human beings but chosen and precious to God (2:4). His followers are invited to be living stones also, built into God's spiritual house to be a holy priesthood to offer acceptable spiritual sacrifices to God through Christ (2:5).

Such a reading affirms the priesthood of all Christians, not that everyone is his or her own priest, but that each is a priest to others. To offer sacrifice (the word comes from two words meaning to "make holy" or to "make whole") as a priest means to be an instrument to make relationships with God and others whole in the spirit of God's whole-making deed in Christ.

The reading grounds the image of the stone in several texts from Israel's Scriptures. Applied now to Jesus, faith in him as God's precious cornerstone (Isaiah 28:16; Psalm 118:22) does not lead to stumbling on the stone and falling (Isaiah 8:14–15). The writer links Israel's Scriptures to faith in Jesus Christ.

To develop further the communal character of God's spiritual house, the writer turns to more images in Israel's history. Believers in Jesus now are a chosen race, a royal priesthood, a holy nation (Exodus 19:6), God's own people (Hosea 2:23).

These names are not ends in themselves. They are for the purpose of proclaiming God's mighty acts that called them "out of darkness into God's marvelous light" (1 Peter 2:9). Once no people and without the blessing of mercy, now they are God's people with mercy (2:10).

Our baptism also makes us first recipients and then agents of God's mercy. As a race, priesthood, and nation now we are to break barriers so all people may know that they are God's people.

Respond to the Word

- Whom will you invite to join the fellowship of God's people?
- What steps do you need to take this week to grow toward greater spiritual maturity as one of God's people?

Go with the Word

Arthur Boyd, *Moses Leading the People, 1947* (Australia, 1920–   ). Used
by permission of the Bundanon Trust, New South Wales, Australia.

    The words of 1 Peter 2 recall God's saving act, Moses and the
Exodus. The covenant between God and the people established the
Hebrews as God's own. The writer of First Peter identifies the
church as a continuation of "the people of God."

1. Henri J. M. Nouwen, *Out of Solitude: Three Meditations on the Christian
Life* (Notre Dame, Ind.: Ave Maria Press, 1974), 21, 22, 23–24.

Because I Live, You Live

Jesus said, "In a little while the world will no longer see me, but you will see me; because I live, you also will live. On that day you will know that I am in God, and you in me, and I in you."

John 14:19–20

Bible Reading: John 14:15–21

Additional Bible Readings: Acts 17:22–31/Psalm 66:8–20
1 Peter 3:13–22

Enter the Word

- What hope does Jesus' resurrection give to humanity?
- What do you believe about the power of the resurrection?

Think about the sights and sounds that bring feelings of desolation or grief to your mind.

Now read John 14:15–21. At the moment that Jesus is talking to the disciples, he is describing the emptiness and the great personal loss they may feel when he leaves them. He tells them that he is leaving, but that this is not the end of their relationship. He assures them that he will not leave them desolate. He is describing his death and his resurrection—and the coming of the Spirit, who will comfort them and is to comfort us. Jesus wanted the disciples to understand that the crucifixion event was part of God's plan and that it was not the end, but the beginning.

Jesus is telling the disciples that he will rise from the dead for the salvation of all. He says that the Spirit of God, which was also in him, will be with us always.

Jesus is revealing the powerful message of the resurrection; he will leave—will go through death and resurrection—so that all will inherit eternal life. These words have the power to dispel desolation. Jesus has made the promise. As God was in him, so God is in Christians' hearts. The Spirit of God will come to believers as the Comforter through life and take them beyond death. Meditate on this message of resurrection and how it may affect your life.

Also read Paul's message to the Athenians, found in Acts 17:22–31. The psalmist offers praise for God's care of the people in Psalm 66:8–20. Just as Jesus suffered, 1 Peter 3:13–22 reminds believers that they too may suffer for their faith.

> *Thanks be to God, for I live because Christ is alive by the power of the resurrection. Amen.*

Engage the Word

- What help might John's community have needed in understanding the resurrection and discovering its power for their lives?

John 14:15–21 is part of Jesus' farewell discourse at the Last Supper in the Gospel of John (chapters 13–17). Unlike the other Gospels, there were no "words of institution" at the meal, but there was a foot washing (13:3–15). In light of his coming death and departure from this world, Jesus interpreted the meaning of his leaving the disciples and sought to prepare them for their life after he was gone from them physically.

But in John's Gospel, these words of Jesus no longer address the first disciples some sixty years earlier; instead, they address John's community. John shapes the story to meet their needs. The first generation of Christians had expected Jesus' return and the world's end in their lifetime, but now history had moved on into the second and third generations. These believers were asking how long they must wait for Jesus' coming.

The reading from John 14 helps to answer that question by telling of the *parakletos*, which can be translated as "the one called alongside," the Advocate, the Counselor, the Comforter. This name for the Holy Spirit is unique to John's Gospel. Jesus promised to those who love and keep God's commandments that God would send the Paraclete to be with them forever after Jesus was gone (John 14:15–16; see also 14:26; 15:26; 16:7; 13:34; 15:12, 17). This Paraclete is the "Spirit of truth" (14:17), the truth of God's love in Jesus.

Those in the world who do not love both Jesus and one another cannot receive or know the Paraclete, but the disciples who do love will know the Paraclete's abiding presence. Also, that presence brings the presence of Jesus. He says, "I will not leave you orphaned; I am coming to you" (14:18).

John's community does not have to wait for some future coming of the risen Jesus. Through the Paraclete, the Holy Spirit and God will come to them and make their home with them (14:23). With their spiritual eyes, they will "see" the risen Jesus; and the life that is in him will be life in them (14:19).

The Holy Spirit brings a mutuality of in-dwelling: Jesus in God, the disciples in Jesus, and Jesus in the disciples (14:20). This inter-relationship is one of keeping Jesus' commandment to love—the disciples love Jesus, both Jesus and God love them, and Jesus reveals himself to them in love (14:21).

Neither John's community in the first century nor believers in our day need to wait for Jesus' coming. He comes every day to those who love him and keep his commandment to love. The life that is in him becomes life in us, life that is God's gift of love in Jesus. We love because God first loved us. Our love is a response to God's love for us, and our life becomes a life of love for others.

Psalm 66 speaks of the God "who has kept us among the living" (66:9) and who has not "removed God's steadfast love" (66:20). First Peter calls readers to "turn away from evil and do good . . . seek peace and pursue it" (3:11). To do this is to love and by the Spirit to know the life of Jesus at work in us.

Respond to the Word

- With whom can you share the comforting words of John 14?
- Where do you need the liberating power of the resurrection to work in your own life? How will you open yourself to that power?

Go with the Word

Whatever else the disciples would come to understand about what had happened, they knew from the start that the resurrection was not simply about what happened to Jesus; it is about what happens to all who trust in Jesus, and about what can happen to all who claim this story as their own. The resurrection is not simply the assurance that Jesus was victorious over death; it is also a promise that we can share in that victory with him. The resurrection does not mean only that Jesus was triumphant over evil; it also assures us that evil will not be ultimately triumphant in our own lives. The resurrection is a promise offered to all. Saint Jean Vianney said of Easter, "Today one grave is open, and from it has risen a sun which will never be obscured, which will never set, a sun which bestows new life."

Martin B. Copenhaver, *To Begin at the Beginning: An Introduction to the Christian Faith* (Cleveland: United Church Press, 1994), 57. Used by permission.

Steadfast in Faith

Cast all your anxieties on God, because God cares for you.

1 Peter 5:7

Bible Reading: 1 Peter 4:12–14, 5:6–11

Additional Bible Readings: Acts 1:6–14/
                                      Psalm 68:1–10, 32–35
                                      John 17:1–11

Enter the Word

- What does it mean to be "steadfast" in your faith?
- What cares do you need to cast on God right now?

Write down the worries that you are struggling with today. As you read 1 Peter 5:7, ask God to help you feel more peaceful. Now tear up your list of anxieties and cast it aside.

We all know that many cares cannot be cast aside quite so easily. Yet, Henri Nouwen implies that at least some of our anxiety is self-inflicted. In *Making All Things New*, he writes:

> More enslaving than our occupations, however, are our preoccupations. To be pre-occupied means to fill our time and place long before we are there. . . . It is a mind filled with "ifs.". . . All these "ifs" fill our minds with anxious thoughts and make us wonder constantly what to do and what to say in case something should happen in the future. Much, if not most, of our suffering is connected with these preoccupations. . . . Since we are always preparing for eventualities, we seldom fully trust the moment.[1]

Read 1 Peter 4:12–14 and 5:6–11. Peter writes to a community that has good reason for some of their fears (see "Engage the

Word"), yet he too advises trust. Being "steadfast in their faith" will help them deal with the fears and anxieties that threaten their peace.

Reflect on how developing an attitude of basic trust improves your life. Consider how trusting that God will "restore, support, strengthen, and establish you" (1 Peter 5:10) helps you to cast away unnecessary worries and cope better with genuine concerns.

As you read the passages from Acts, Psalm 68, and John, be alert for ways that they connect to the idea of trusting God with cares.

> *I cast my cares on you, O God, trusting that you will empower me to deal with the problems that beset me. Amen.*

Engage the Word

- How might 1 Peter have helped readers cope with anxieties regarding persecution for their faith?

The scripture reading for Easter 5 was also from 1 Peter (see "Engage the Word"). That reading may have been part of a baptismal sermon incorporated into a letter. Today's scripture is part of the letter that follows that sermon and speaks to a situation of persecution and suffering. That suffering may have been either under the emperor Nero in the sixties, Domitian in the nineties, or Trajan in the second century, but the time of Domitian seems the most likely.

The writer distinguished among different kinds of suffering. Suffering for the cause of Christ would stem from refusing to worship the emperor. That suffering should come as no surprise (1 Peter 4:12). This suffering would correspond to Christ's suffering for God's cause (4:13). Suffering justly for crimes committed is something else (4:15).

Suffering as a Christian in the present will lead to glory and joy in the future, and being reviled for the name of Christ means the blessing of God's Spirit is upon you (compare the Beatitudes in Matthew 5:10–12). Short-term suffering for Christ will lead to long-term glory from God, but the spirit of blessing already rests on those who suffer for their faith.

Today's scripture then skips from 1 Peter 4:14 to 5:6. The material between these passages has to do with judgment, with God's household, and with an appeal to its leaders.

After lifting up the need for humility and proclaiming God's favor on the humble, the writer exhorts, "Humble yourselves therefore under the mighty hand of God, so that God may exalt you in due time" (1 Peter 5:6). This view contrasted with that of the emperor who exalted himself. (Domitian wanted to be known as "our Lord and God.") Christians know that the ultimate "mighty hand" is God's, not the emperor's. Humility before God is what finally counts.

Then comes, "Cast all your anxieties on God, because God cares for you" (5:7). In persecution, anxiety would run high. People needed to know that the caring hand of God was with them.

Such circumstances called for discipline and resistance to face the devouring forces of evil, pictured as the devil and a "roaring lion" (5:8). The Revelation of John also deals with persons facing Roman persecution. John associated satan ("satan" is Hebrew; "devil" is Greek) and the beast with Rome and called for resistance to the idolatry of making the emperor and Rome one's first loyalty. In 1 Peter the lion symbolized Roman political power.

The situation called for being "steadfast in your faith." The ones 1 Peter addressed were not alone; others around the Roman Empire were suffering the same (5:9). First Peter calls readers to contrast their temporary suffering with the grace and gift of God's eternal glory. God will take care of them. Therefore, to God—not the emperor or anyone else—belongs the power forever (5:11).

Psalm 68 calls for scattering the enemy (68:1) and praising the God who cares for orphans, widows (68:5), prisoners (68:6), and the needy (68:10) and who gives power and strength (68:35).

Respond to the Word

- How can you help others learn to trust in God so that they are better able to cope with their cares?
- What anxieties will you turn over to God right now?

Go with the Word

Night Prayer

It is night.
The night is for stillness.
  Let us be still in the presence of God.

It is night after a long day.
  What has been done has been done;
  what has not been done has not been done;
  let it be.

The night is dark.
  Let our fears of the darkness of the world and of our own lives
  rest in you.

The night is quiet.
  Let the quietness of your peace enfold us,
    all dear to us,
    and all who have no peace.

The night heralds the dawn.
  Let us look expectantly to a new day,
    new joys,
    new possibilities.

In your name we pray.
Amen.

"Night Prayer" (excerpt), in *A New Zealand Prayer Book: He Karakia Mihinare o Aotearoa* (Auckland, New Zealand: William Collins Publishers, Ltd., 1989), 184. This copyrighted material is used by permission.

1. Henri J. M. Nouwen, *Making All Things New* (San Francisco: Harper and Row, 1981), 25–26.

Paul Gauguin, *Vision after the Sermon (Jacob Wrestling with the Angel)*,
1888, National Gallery of Scotland, Edinburgh, Great Britain
(Bridgeman Art Library International, Ltd., London/New York). Used
by permission.

Pentecost

Following the earth-changing event of God's gift of the Holy Spirit being poured out, the season after Pentecost is a time to nurture the Spirit within so as to grow steadily in the faith. During this long stretch that extends to Advent, altars are covered with green to symbolize growth. This season is known as ordinary time because no major festivals of the church year occur.

Disciples encounter not only heady spiritual moments of growth but also quiet times of rest as Jesus promised. The Sunday following Pentecost provides time to learn what the dominion of God is all about. Moreover, this season challenges Christ's followers to sow the seed of God's word so that others may come to believe. Like Jacob, those who seek to know God's will for their lives must struggle as individuals. But life among God's people is not a solitary journey, for believers are called to live pleasantly together in community, offering hospitality to all. Within this body, the faithful not only find their place but leave their indelible marks as they use the gifts and talents God has endowed them with to build up the church.

Look at the picture *Vision after the Sermon (Jacob Wrestling with the Angel)*. Ponder the ways you are wrestling with yourself, with others, and with God. How have your struggles empowered you to grow as a Christian disciple? How have they made the presence of God more real in your life?

Filled with the Spirit

When the day of Pentecost had come, they were all together in one place. All of them were filled with the Holy Spirit and began to speak in other languages, as the Spirit gave them ability.

Acts 2:1, 4

Bible Reading: Acts 2:1–21

Additional Bible Readings: Psalm 104:24–34, 35b
1 Corinthians 12:3b–13
John 20:19–23

Enter the Word

- In what ways might an indwelling of the Spirit change lives?
- What experiences have you had that indicated the presence of God's Spirit in your life?

As you read Acts 2:1–21, look for the descriptions of a remarkable experience of the presence and power of God's Holy Spirit. Think about the disciples coming together in one accord with their common love of Jesus. Reflect on this unity.

The experience of God's presence and power is expressed as the sound of a wind and the tongues of fire. Perhaps you have had an experience of God that you had difficulty expressing in words. Recall or imagine an experience of God's presence, perhaps one that occurred on a typical day as you went about your ordinary routine.

Witnesses to the Pentecost experience had no way to understand what they saw and heard. Ponder what it means to you for God to "pour out" the Holy Spirit on all flesh.

Being saved suggests a number of ideas in addition to "rescue"—being healed, protected, delivered, made whole by a power greater than our own. Remember ways you have experienced the power of God's Holy Spirit to save, heal, or make you whole.

As you read the passages from Psalm 104, 1 Corinthians, and John, be aware of the gift and power of God's Spirit.

> *Fill me with your Spirit that I may be made whole.*
> *Amen.*

Engage the Word

- How might Luke's story of Pentecost have empowered his own community for witness and service?

Luke narrates the exciting story of the momentous formation of the church at Pentecost as a powerful work of God's Holy Spirit. He has already highlighted the empowering work of the Spirit in Jesus' ministry in the Gospel of Luke (Luke 1:34–35; 4:1–2; 10:21–22). In fact, the centrality of the power of the Holy Spirit in Jesus' life and ministry *and* in the life of the early church is of major importance to Luke, both in the Gospel of Luke and the Acts of the Apostles.

Pentecost, one of the great annual festivals of the Jews, fell on the fiftieth day after Passover (Leviticus 23:15–16). Thousands of pilgrims traveled from all over the world to worship in the Jerusalem Temple and to offer the first fruits of their labor in accordance with Jewish custom.

"When the day of Pentecost had come, they were all together in one place" (Acts 2:1). This scene of the disciples gathered together in one place must be understood in light of Luke 24:49, where Jesus had charged them: "Stay here in the city until you have been clothed with power from on high." Jesus was departing, but the Holy Spirit would come to God's people on earth in his place. They would never be alone! The Spirit would lead and empower them for the journey of faith.

A dramatic event occurred on the day of Pentecost. The

promised Holy Spirit descended with a sound like the rush of a mighty wind. The miraculous power of the Holy Spirit was visible in the brilliant tongues of fire that rested upon them. The wonders continued as they were filled with the Holy Spirit and spoke in other languages about the mighty acts of God as the Spirit enabled them (Acts 2:11).

The vision and sound of this event attracted a curious, amazed, and bewildered multitude (Acts 2:5–6). Peter's spontaneous and informative sermon provided the interpretive glue that they needed to make sense of the puzzle before them. God's outpouring of the gift of the Holy Spirit had been foretold by the prophet Joel (Joel 2:28–32). All humankind would recognize Pentecost as the day God brought the new age of the church fully into being.

What does it mean to experience the empowerment of the Holy Spirit? Luke provides a diverse and rich mosaic of the Holy Spirit's actions in the lives of Christians in Acts. Above all, the Holy Spirit confirms God's presence and power in the church, and the Holy Spirit equips believers to witness boldly (Acts 1:8; 2:17–18; 4:1–31). The Holy Spirit makes the unity of the church visible in loving, nurturing, and sacrificial community interactions of Christian men and women (4:32–37; 9:36–43; 20:17–36). In short, being "filled with the Spirit" means being empowered to live a life that is a sign of Christ's joyous presence and salvation.

The additional scripture passages for today illumine the breadth and magnitude of the Holy Spirit's work in all of creation (Psalm 104:24–34, 35b) and in the diverse distribution and empowerment of gifts in the life of the church (1 Corinthians 12:3b–13; John 20:19–23). Pentecost represented a decisive turning point in the history of God's saving deeds.

Respond to the Word

- Where will you allow God's Spirit to work through you to witness to others this week?
- Read "Exuberant Spirit of God." What changes does this poem call you to make in your own life?

Go with the Word

Exuberant Spirit of God

Exuberant Spirit of God,
bursting with the brightness of flame
into the coldness of our lives
to warm us with a passion for justice and beauty,
we praise you.

Exuberant Spirit of God,
sweeping us out of the dusty corners of our apathy
to breathe vitality into our struggles for change,
we praise you.

Exuberant Spirit of God,
speaking words that leap over barriers of mistrust
to convey messages of truth and new understanding,
we praise you.

Exuberant Spirit of God,
    flame
        wind
            speech,
burn, breathe, speak in us;
fill your world with justice and with joy.

Jan Berry, in *Bread of Tomorrow: Prayers for the Church Year*, ed. Janet
Morley (Maryknoll, N.Y.: Orbis Books, 1992), 129. Used by permission.

And It Was Good

God saw everything that God had made, and indeed, it was very good.

Genesis 1:31a

Bible Reading: Genesis 1:1–2:4a

Additional Bible Readings: Psalm 8
                            2 Corinthians 13:11–13
                            Matthew 28:16–20

Enter the Word

- Why do you think God pronounced all creation "good"?
- How do you enjoy and celebrate the goodness of creation?

Read Genesis 1:1–2:4a leisurely, preferably outdoors. Pause after reading each day's narration. Think about ways you can you see, touch, hear, smell, or taste that day's created miracle in the environment immediately around you.

Move beyond simply *thinking* about the reading's connection to your particular place—experience it. Run your hand along a tree's rough bark. Sniff a newly opened flower. Listen to a bird's song. Let your eyes perceive varying shades of light. Bite into a piece of fresh fruit. Experience creation's gifts.

Now sit back and rest your eyes and body. Remember each one of the biblical days of creation; not by the words in Genesis but by the gifts God created. Recall the refrain pronounced after each day's work: "And God saw that it was good." Offer a prayer of thanks for God's creation and for the goodness you find in each of its day's bounties.

Also consider how human attitude or action could possibly mar or deny the goodness of God's creation. Think about ways you have experienced the impact of disregard for creation's goodness (e.g., pollution, wasteful use of resources, racism). Recall how you have responded to your experience(s).

Read the additional scriptures and see what connections you can draw between them and the passage from Genesis.

> *Thanks be to you, O God, for the gifts of creation I am privileged to experience. Amen.*

Engage the Word

- What does the creation story reveal about God the Creator?

"In the beginning . . . God created . . ." These words in Genesis 1:1 highlight two awe-inspiring and incontestable truths. First, the opening words of scripture emphasize the Eternal One who is without beginning or end, *God.*

> *Before the mountains were*
> *brought forth,*
> *or ever you had formed the*
> *earth and the world,*
> *from everlasting to everlasting,*
> *you are God. (Psalm 90:2)*

God alone existed in the beginning. The writer of the Gospel of John in the New Testament reiterates this theme when John records Jesus' words in the prayer uttered before his crucifixion: "Father, I desire that those also, whom you have given me, may be with me where I am, to see my glory, which you have given me because you loved me before the foundation of the world" (John 17:24).[1]

If the first inexhaustible truth about Genesis 1:1 is the affirmation of God's primacy, the second is the origin and dependence of all creation upon God: "God created the heavens and the earth."

The Hebrew Scriptures use the word "created" (in Hebrew, *bara*) in reference to God only. God creates, bringing the universe into existence *ex nihilo*, from nothing. Paul the Apostle reiterates this assertion when he speaks to the Roman Christians about God "who gives life to the dead and calls into existence the things that do not exist" (Romans 4:17b). A careful review of the six days of creation (Genesis 1:5, 8, 13, 19, 23, 31) suggests that creation progressed from a state of nothingness through a state of formlessness and emptiness to a condition where the formlessness gave way to "form" and the emptiness surrendered to "fullness."[2] The eternal God did not make, manufacture, or construct (with existing materials) but called into being the material elements of the universe.

God's creation of the universe by the word of God's own command occurs in a dramatic flurry of activity in Genesis 1:1–2:4a. Light bursts forth and is separated from darkness; the firmament divides the waters from the waters; the sky stands like a great canopy over the whole earth; and sprouting, fruit-bearing vegetation lavishly covers the landscape. Living creatures of every kind traverse the sea. The earth is alive with creeping animals and the sky alive with winged birds in flight (1:3–25).

God's crowning achievement was the creation of humankind— male and female—in God's own image. God blessed (1:28) and equipped humanity to act as God's people in the earth (1:28–30).

Genesis 1:31a accentuates a recurrent refrain in Genesis 1:1– 2:4a: creation is good. This affirmation that the work of God's hands is "good" interlaces throughout the catalogue of elements that God brings into being (1:4, 10b, 12b, 18b, 21b, 25b). As the omnipotent Creator surveys the whole sweep of the created cosmos, God's pleasure is unmistakably clear: "God saw everything that God had made, and indeed, it was very good" (1:31a).

A cosmic litany of praise and thanksgiving, as found in Psalm 8, is an appropriate response to reflection on God, our Creator.

Respond to the Word

- What would it take to affirm and protect God's good creation?
- How will you work with others to be good stewards of God's creation?

Go with the Word

An African Canticle

> *All you big things, bless the Lord*
> *Mount Kilimanjaro and Lake Victoria*
> *The Rift Valley and the Serengeti Plain*
> *Fat baobabs and shady mango trees*
> *All eucalyptus and tamarind trees*
> *Bless the Lord*
> *Praise and extol [God] for ever and ever.*
>
> *All you tiny things, bless the Lord*
> *Busy black ants and hopping fleas*
> *Wriggling tadpoles and mosquito larvae*
> *Flying locusts and water drops*
> *Pollen dust and tsetse flies*
> *Millet seeds and dried dagaa*
> *Bless the Lord*
> *Praise and extol [God] for ever and ever.*

From *Earth Prayers from Around the World*, ed. Elizabeth Roberts and Elias Amidon (San Francisco: Harper San Francisco, 1991), 219. Used by permission of the Church Mission Society.

1. See also John 1:1–10 on the preexistence of the Word.
2. D. Stuart Briscoe, *Genesis: The Communicator's Commentary* (Waco, Tex.: Word, 1986), 36.

Doers of God

Not everyone who says to me, "Lord, Lord," will enter the dominion of heaven, but only the one who does the will of my Father and Mother in heaven. Everyone then who hears these words of mine and acts on them will be like a wise one who built a house on rock.

Matthew 7:21, 24

Bible Reading: Matthew 7:21–29

Additional Bible Readings: Genesis 6:9–22, 7:24, 8:14–19/
                                    Psalm 46
                                or Deuteronomy 11:18–21, 26–28/
                                    Psalm 31:1–5, 19–24
                                  Romans 1:16–17, 3:22b–28 (29–31)

Enter the Word

- What are some actions one might take to be a "doer of God"?
- In what ways are you are "doer of God"?

Think back over the last twenty-four hours. Recall any actions that you took because you thought God wanted you to do them.

Now read Matthew 7:21–29. Try to envision a house built on solid rock, perhaps located atop a mountain, as well as a house built on sand, possibly located at water's edge in a beach resort town. Picture in your mind a fierce storm pounding both of these homes. See one standing firm and the other disintegrating into the ocean. Draw parallels between this image and your own spiritual condition. Meditate on how you act on God's words. See if you can add new possibilities to your list of actions on behalf of God.

As you read Deuteronomy 11:18–21, 26–28, look for ways that this passage echoes Jesus' teaching in Matthew 7. Paul's writing to the church at Rome speaks about righteousness that calls forth faith in God's redemptive work through Christ. In seeking deliverance from enemies, the writer of Psalm 31 expresses confidence in God, his "rock of refuge" (31:2).

Help me not only to hear but to act on your words. Amen.

Engage the Word

- What practical implications of Jesus' message are set forth in the close of the Sermon on the Mount?

Today's Bible reading is another text from the Sermon on the Mount. For some introduction to Matthew's Gospel, see the first two paragraphs under "Engage the Word" for Proper 2.

In Matthew 7, after teachings about judging and critiquing others (7:1–5), indiscriminate giving (7:6), asking, searching, knocking (7:7–11), the Golden Rule (7:12), narrow and wide gates (7:13–14), false prophets (7:15), and good and bad fruit (7:16–20), Jesus makes a decisive statement about just who will enter into God's dominion: "Not everyone who says to me, 'Lord, Lord,' will enter the dominion of heaven, but those who do the will of my Father and Mother who is in heaven" (7:21).

The test will not be a matter of verbal confession, even the central one among early Christians, "Jesus Christ is Lord." The test is *doing* God's will, not just talking the talk but walking the walk. It is those who do God's will who are Jesus' "brother and sister and mother" (12:50; see also 21:28–31).

Jesus taught his disciples to pray, "Your will be done, on earth as it is in heaven" (Matthew 6:10). Jesus himself had to struggle with what God's will was for him as he faced death: "God my Father and Mother, if it be possible, let this cup pass from me; yet not what I want but what you want" (26:39). God's will for him was an uncompromising mission of "justice and mercy and faith" (23:23), even if it led to crucifixion at the hands of threatened religious and political leaders.

At the last judgment, who is it that will inherit God's realm? It is those who have fed the hungry, given drink to the thirsty, welcomed the stranger, clothed the naked, cared for the sick, and visited those in prison (Matthew 25:35–36). This is doing the will of God. Jesus rejects those who simply use Jesus' name to prophesy, cast out demons, and do deeds of power (7:22–23).

As the Sermon on the Mount moves toward the end, Jesus calls his disciples not only to *hear* his words but to *act* on them (7:24). Those who hear and do his words are like the wise person who builds a house on solid rock. Those who hear them and do not do them are like a foolish person who builds on shifting sand (7:24–27).

The reading from Deuteronomy also shows a major concern for words (11:18–21, 26–28). But God's blessing falls on those who *obey* God's commandments, who *do* the words (11:27). Further, the Psalm reading also uses the image of the rock in prayer, "You are indeed my rock" (Psalm 31:3).

The Sermon on the Mount comes to an end with its hearers "astonished at his teaching" and with an assertion of Jesus' authority (Matthew 7:28–29). The new Moses has spoken, not with some secondary footnoting like the scribes, the religious teachers. His was a primary authority, the authority of one who not only spoke about the will of God but who embodied it and did it, even unto death. This is the One to whose words Matthew called his first readers, and now us, to listen to and act upon if we want to do God's will and enter God's realm.

For Paul, the heart of the gospel is this climax of Jesus' death and resurrection. God's love in Jesus' obedience made many right with God (Romans 5:8, 19). The apostle calls this salvation (1:16), justification as grace and gift, redemption, atonement (3:24–25), pregnant *words* about the result of the One who did the loving will of God.

Respond to the Word

- Who do you know whose spiritual home is built on sand? How can you help this person to move to solid ground with God?
- What will you do in response to Jesus' teaching this week?

Go with the Word

What Will You Do?

When I come in the guise
of the needy, the helpless,
the cold and the hungry,
the stranger, the lonely,
will you look away?
    What will you do?
    What will you say?

When I come close to home
in the need of your neighbor,
at times inconvenient,
in places and faces
that mask and conceal me . . .
    What will you do?
    What will you say?

When I come in the message
of prophet and preacher,
in truths inescapable
or words which dismay,
will you listen to me
and give me a welcome?
    What will you do?
    What will you say?

When, face to face
at the end of the journey,
we look at each other,
will you look away?
    What will you do?
    What will you say?

Kenneth Carveley, *All Year Round* (British Council of Churches, 1988), in *Bread of Tomorrow: Prayers for the Church Year*, ed. Janet Morley (Maryknoll, N.Y.: Orbis Books, 1992), 26.

You Will Be a Blessing

Now God said to Abram, "Go from your country and your kindred and your parents' house to the land that I will show you. I will make of you a great nation, and I will bless you, and make your name great, so that you will be a blessing and in you all the families of the earth shall be blessed." So Abram went, as God had told him.

Genesis 12:1–2, 3b–4a

Bible Reading: Genesis 12:1–9

Additional Bible Readings: Psalm 33:1–12
                                         or Hosea 5:15–6:6/Psalm 50:7–15
                                         Romans 4:13–25
                                         Matthew 9:9–13, 18–26

Enter the Word

- How has God blessed you?
- How do you see yourself as a blessing to others?

Listen to what God might be saying to you as you read about Abram and Sarai's response to God's call as found in Genesis 12:1–9. God promises to bless Abram so that he will be a blessing to others. The Hebrew word for blessing, *berakah*, suggests good words and intentions. It is associated with the idea of prosperity. The root of the word means "to kneel," a way of showing honor or respect for someone. God promises to honor Abram with good in order that Abram might honor or "bless" others with good.

List the ways God has honored or blessed you. Identify your feelings when you recognize and name God's blessings. Recall the ways have you blessed others as a result of God's blessings to you. Consider additional ways that you could be a blessing to others.

Abram and Sarai were called to journey to a new land and to make a new life when Abram was seventy-five years old. Traveling and resettling at any age is challenging, and to do so in one's later years demonstrates that faith and obedience to God can move one beyond the limitations of an aging body. Abram and Sarai journeyed on foot with all their animals, servants, tents, and possessions.

Like Abram and Sarai, our obedient response to God can move us beyond what we see as our limits. Think about your life as a journey. Remember where you have been and envision where you think you are going. Reflect on the enjoyable moments and the distressing moments. Recall the ways God was with you and moved you beyond your limitations.

Think about ways your life journey has been a blessing to others. Open your mind and heart to God's presence now.

As you study the other passages for today, link them to the reading from Genesis.

> *With great joy, I give thanks for the ways you have blessed me, O God, and allowed me to be a blessing to others. Amen.*

Engage the Word

- How would the story of Abram and Sarai have helped the covenant people to experience God's blessings?

"You will be a blessing" (Genesis 12:2c). God's promise to Abram foretold the unfolding of events of universal and monumental importance. God's covenant with Abram would lead to blessing for all of the families of the earth.

God is the agent and source of Abram's blessing and greatness. Attentive readers of Genesis 12:1–9 will notice the startling recurrence of the "I wills" in God's charge to Abram. Abram and his kindred should go to the land "that I will show you" (12:1). "I will make of you a great nation, and I will bless you" (12:2). "I will bless those who bless you, and the one who curses you I will curse" (12:3). "To your offspring I will give this land" (12:7). It was God who had promised, and God would bring it to pass! God was faithful and gracious in fulfilling the divine promise.

Abraham's faith was a trusting faith. The writer of Hebrews includes Abraham in the "Hall of Faith"—the catalog of heroes of faith who trusted God's faithfulness (Hebrews 11:1–39). In fact, Abraham is listed twice as an active pioneer of faith (Hebrews 11:8–12, 17–19). Abraham knew that God could be trusted. Leaving everything behind, he moved boldly into the new future to which God was calling him, knowing neither where he was going nor the trials and challenges that awaited him.

Abraham's faith was a personal faith. He recognized Yahweh (a Hebrew name for God) as his God. Abraham's son Isaac later heard these comforting words: "I am the God of your father Abraham" (Genesis 26:24). God appeared to Abraham (12:7, 17:1, 18:1), and Abraham knew God as "God Most High, maker of heaven and earth" (14:22), his "shield" (15:1), and "the Everlasting God" (21:33).

Abraham's faith was a covenant faith. A covenant (the Hebrew *berith*) is a formal agreement or treaty between two or more parties with each assuming some obligation. God's call of Abraham culminated in the fulfillment of God's divine plan of salvation for all humankind through Abraham and Sarah's descendants, for the lineage of Jesus the Messiah would be traced back to Abraham (Matthew 1:1).

Those who would hear and experience God's promise of blessing are called to exhibit the same kind of personal, trusting confidence in God's purposes and promise as Abraham. Psalm 33 states that the nation whose God is the creator and ruler of history is happy, that is, blessed.

Those who have faith in Jesus Christ join the descendants of Abraham and Sarah, for their faith, like Abraham's, will be "reckoned to them as righteousness" (Romans 4:13–25).

Respond to the Word

- How can members of your church bless and support one another?
- What can you do today to thank God for your blessings?

Go with the Word

Blessed Are You

Blessed are you,
God of growth and discovery;
yours is the inspiration
that has altered and changed our lives;
yours is the power that has brought us
to new dangers and opportunities.
Set us, your new creation,
to walk through this new world, watching and learning,
loving and trusting,
until your kingdom comes.

Amen.

"Prayer Number 3," in *A New Zealand Prayer Book: He Karakia Mihinare o Aotearoa* (Auckland, New Zealand: William Collins Publishers, Ltd., 1989). This copyrighted material is used by permission.

L a u g h   w i t h   M e

Abraham was a hundred years old when his son Isaac was born to him. Now Sarah said, "God has brought laughter for me; everyone who hears will laugh with me."

Genesis 21:5–6

Bible Reading: Genesis 18:1–15 (21:1–7)

Additional Bible Readings: Psalm 116:1–2, 12–19
                                                            or Exodus 19:2–8a/Psalm 100
                                                            Romans 5:1–8
                                                            Matthew 9:35–10:8 (9–23)

Enter the Word

- What does the ability to laugh say about a person?
- What prompts you to laugh?

Reflect on the occasions and causes for laughter in your own life. Visualize times of joy and laughter in your family, at your work, with friends, or with your faith community. Hear again that laughter and recall the joy that prompted it.

Read Genesis 18:1–5 (21:1–7). Remember a time that you had a promise fulfilled unexpectedly and reflect on your feelings. You may have believed that the person had forgotten about the promise or maybe you had forgotten it. Perhaps the unexpectedness made you feel more grateful that the promise was fulfilled.

Now think of a time when someone came to you with news that you could hardly believe. Recall your reaction to that person's

news. Maybe you reacted by laughing when you were actually
embarrassed, or nervous, or even frightened, rather than amused.
Consider why Sarah might have laughed.

Just imagine her predicament. She waited *decades* for the child
God had promised. She certainly knew she was past childbearing
age—her biological clock had run out years ago. And after all this
time she would have a baby, *now*. She laughed to herself when she
heard this seemingly incredible news (Genesis 18:12). It wasn't dis-
respect. She must have decided a long time before that God
intended to fulfill that promise in some other way. She probably
never expected to hear about it again.

Later, Sarah says, "everyone who hears will laugh with me"
(21:6). She is referring to us, too. Sarah is proof that God's promises are fulfilled when we least expect them. Sarah is also proof that
God can overcome humanity's physical limitations when the time
is right.

Try to put yourself in Sarah's place. Imagine the doubt and fear
that probably accompanied her joy at God's promise of a child, fulfilled after so many years.

Be sure to read the additional scriptures and reflect on them.

> *I laugh, O God, when I recall with joy the many promis-
> es you have fulfilled in my life, often in unexpected ways.
> Amen.*

Engage the Word

- What does Sarah's response to the fulfilled promise of a
  child say to the readers about her understanding of God?

"God has brought laughter for me; everyone who hears will
laugh with me" (Genesis 21:6). Sarah's utterance reflects her
incredulity, her pure joy, at the miracle that God had wrought in
her life: she gave birth to a son, Isaac. Long accustomed to barren-
ness, the idea that she could experience motherhood in the latter
years of her life was beyond her wildest imagination. But God had
blessed Sarah and Abraham with a son, fulfilling the divine
promise that Abraham's descendants would be "as numerous as the
stars of heaven and as the sand that is on the seashore" (22:17).
Nothing is impossible with God (18:14)!

"Laugh with me." Sarah's words remind us of a profoundly real theological truth: God bestows gifts and blessings on humankind in often startling and unexpected ways. From a biblical and theological perspective, laughter is sometimes an appropriate response to the astonishing creativity that God exhibits in fulfilling the divine will. God's ways are often so mysterious and unusual that they provoke laughter from the people of God.

Sarah and Abraham remind us that biblical belief often concerns the "impossible" from a human standpoint. It is important to remember that *both* Abraham and Sarah laughed at the idea that God would bless them with a son. (Abraham laughs in 17:17; Sarah in 18:12.)

The acknowledgment and enjoyment of God's unexpected gifts may evoke unrestrained laughter and joy. "When people plan, trusting only in human power, God laughs; when God plans, working through human weakness, people laugh."[1] In fact, it is often the case that unless we "expect the unexpected" on the journey of faith, we will miss the astonishment and joy that God's gracious actions in our lives will disclose.

This lesson's title, "Laugh with Me," is an invitation for the community of witnesses to God's infinite goodness to join in corporate celebration and thanksgiving. Sarah expects others to hear the good news of Isaac's birth and to join in communal laughter and rejoicing with her. The miracle that God had accomplished was not "done in a corner" (Acts 26:26). The writer of Psalm 116:14, 16–19, in another of today's readings promises to pay vows to the Lord and offer a sacrifice of thanksgiving "in the presence of all the people." May the whole people of God acknowledge and enjoy God's unexpected gifts with unceasing praise. Let us laugh together.

Respond to the Word

- Who has shared good news with you? How can you celebrate with them?
- How will you acknowledge and enjoy God's gifts this week?

Go with the Word

We can laugh with Sarah over the joy of new life in her.
We can also laugh with joy because of
the promise this new life represents for us.
O God, go with us now,
and help us watch for your unexpected gifts.
Help us laugh with you and with each other
when we find your surprises.
Amen.

The *Inviting Word Older Youth Learner's Guide* (Cleveland, Ohio:
United Church Press, 1995), 92. Used by permission.

1. Joseph Grassi, *God Makes Me Laugh: A New Approach to Luke*
(Wilmington, Del.: Michael Glazier, 1986), 14. See also Psalm 2:2–4.

Baptized into New Life

Therefore we have been buried with Christ by baptism into death, so that, just as Christ was raised from the dead by the glory of God, so we too might walk in newness of life.

Romans 6:4

Bible Reading:	Romans 6:1b–11

Additional Bible Readings:	Genesis 21:8–21/
	   Psalm 86:1–10, 16–17
	or Jeremiah 20:7–13/
	   Psalm 69:7–10 (11–15), 16–18
	Matthew 10:24–39

Enter the Word

- What is your understanding of the purpose of baptism?
- What does baptism mean in your own life?

In Romans 5:12–21 Paul speaks about God's free gift of grace as having "dominion" or "abounding" over sin and death. The remarks about baptism emerge from his argument against the idea of continuing in sin in order to experience God's abounding grace. Read Romans 6:1b–11.

Baptism, which means "being wet with water," is an ancient ritual that symbolizes for Christians God's abounding grace offered through Jesus Christ. Another word for abounding is overflowing. Baptism uses water to symbolize God's grace and love flowing over us, cleansing us, healing us, making us whole, and giving us new

life. Baptism marks the initiation into the family of God. It symbolizes dying to our old ways and rising to new life and new behaviors
in the love of Christ. It reminds us that God forgives us and cleans-
es our spirits through the death and resurrection of Jesus Christ.
Through baptism we recognize that God's grace is a gift. God's
grace and love do not depend upon our actions. Our salvation
comes from God and not from our own efforts.

Relax and try to image water. Maybe you see an ocean, a lake,
or a river. Perhaps you hear the noise of water singing in the rocks
of a mountain stream. You may think of the ways you use water in
your home for bathing, for laundry, for drinking, and for cooking.
Allow visions, sounds, and thoughts of water to surface in your
awareness. Meditate on the ways your understandings and experiences of water broaden your understanding of baptism.

Read the words of Dr. Willimon at the end of this chapter.
Then think about what it means to die to an old way of life and
rise to a new way of life. Consider feelings and actions in your life
that emerge from being alive to God in Jesus Christ.

Remember the symbolism of baptism as you encounter today's
readings from Genesis, Psalm 86 and 69, Jeremiah, and Matthew.

> *As I touch water this day let me recall baptismal waters
> flowing over me so that I may experience new life in you.
> Amen.*

Engage the Word

- How does Paul describe new life for his readers?

Paul's letter to the Christians in Rome was written from
Corinth in 56–57 C.E. While he neither founded the churches in
Rome nor had yet visited them, he was eager to assist the believers
in understanding the significance of the power of the gospel for
faith and life (Romans 1:13, 16).

In Romans 6 Paul addresses possible objections to the doctrine of
God's righteousness as presented in chapters 1–5. He opens with the
question: "Should we continue in sin in order that grace may abound?"
(6:1). Paul anticipated that his affirmation in Romans 5:1–21, stating
that the obedience of Christ decisively overcame the death-dealing
reign of sin and death in humankind, would be misunderstood.

Paul employs diatribe (an intense debate with a real or imaginary opponent) as a rhetorical strategy for clarifying his exhortations. The first question asks: since grace abounded all the more when sin increased, may we continue to live in sin so that God's grace will increase all the more? Paul's passionate response is as sharp and explosive as a shot fired out of a cannon: "By no means! How can we who died to sin go on living in it?" (Romans 6:2). The Greek phrase for "By no means," *mē genoito*, represents one of the strongest ways of expressing an objection or protest in the New Testament. It could be translated "May it never be!" or "Let it not happen!" or "Certainly not!" (See also Romans 3:4 and Galatians 2:17; 3:21.)

Paul's appeal to the symbolism of baptism calls the Roman Christians to respond to the divine imperative for God's people to live a spiritually regenerated and morally disciplined life.

Romans 6:4 shows that those who were baptized into Christ Jesus were baptized into his death. For the baptized one, Jesus Christ has broken decisively and once-for-all-time the power of sin and death (5:12–18). God proves God's unfailing love for us in that while we are yet sinners, Christ died for us (5:8). Then since Christ was raised from the dead by the glory of the God, Christians too are raised "to walk in newness of life" (6:4). Christians are called to exhibit in their lives the real change effected by God's grace. The resurrected Christian is alive to God through Jesus Christ (6:11).

Christians who participate in Christ through baptism are to show by their words and deeds that they are members of the redeemed community of God. For Paul, to walk in newness of life is to bear the fruits of the work of God's Holy Spirit in life (Galatians 5:13–6:10).

Respond to the Word

- What can you and your congregation do to nurture the new life of those who are baptized?
- How will you remember your own baptism? Or, what step could you take this week to explore what baptism means to you?

Go with the Word

Sometimes I wonder, in most of our celebrations of baptism, if we reduce the waters of baptism to a mere sprinkle, and cover it up with rosebuds and lace and talk about cute babies and "God loves you and we love you" because we dare not speak about the strange and wonderful work which is beginning in this child on this day. You know how we always try to avoid *death*.

Baptism is death which leads to life.

William H. Willimon, *Remember Who You Are: Baptism, A Model for Christian Life* (Nashville: The Upper Room, 1980), 103.

Even a Cup of Cold Water

Jesus said, "Whoever welcomes you welcomes me, and whoever welcomes me welcomes the one who sent me and whoever gives even a cup of cold water to one of these little ones in the name of a disciple—truly I tell you, none of these will lose their reward."

Matthew 10:40, 42

Bible Reading: Matthew 10:40–42

Additional Bible Readings: Genesis 22:1–14/Psalm 13
or Jeremiah 28:5–9/
  Psalm 89:1–4, 15–18
Romans 6:12–23

Enter the Word

- How do people extend hospitality to others?
- What acts of hospitality make you feel welcome?

Read Matthew 10:40–42. Notice that verse 40 mentions the word "welcomes" four times. The Greek word is *dechomai*, which suggests "receive" or "accept." Jesus is speaking to the disciples. He is sending them out to offer life, hope, and healing to those who will "accept," "receive," or "welcome" such gifts. The verse describes a bond to God through the act of welcoming. "Whoever welcomes you, welcomes me, and whoever welcomes me, welcomes the one who sent me." The disciples offer the gift of God through Christ. Whoever "receives," "accepts," or "welcomes" them, welcomes God. The act of welcoming expands ever wider like ripples on the surface of a pond.

Welcoming is very closely related to the idea of hospitality. Hospitality is the act of receiving guests with friendliness and kindness. To be hospitable is to favor the health, growth, and comfort of new arrivals. It is to be receptive and open.

Remember a time when someone, perhaps a stranger, was hospitable to you. Recall how gestures of hospitality made you feel.

Think about how God shows you "hospitality." Identify the ways in which God welcomes you. Consider the manner in which you show "hospitality" or "welcome" to God. Search your heart to discern ways you might be more "hospitable" or receptive to God.

Be sure to read today's additional scriptures. Try to relate them to Matthew's message of hospitality.

> *May I welcome others just as you, Loving God, have welcomed and accepted me. Amen.*

Engage the Word

- How might Jesus' words have helped Matthew's community offer hospitality to others in Christ's name?

Travel in the Roman Empire in the first century was brisk and expansive. Well-paved roads provided a far-reaching network of highways that connected remote, rural areas and smaller provinces to the larger, bustling cities. Travelers could find rest, lodging, and the other amenities of hospitality—security, refreshment, comfort, and perhaps the gracious sharing of resources—in everything from cheap, poorly established hotels to more luxurious villas. But the most secure way to travel was to rely on the hospitality of friends, relatives, or other personal contacts.[1]

The socio-historical insight about travel and hospitality in the first-century Greco-Roman world is instructive for understanding the significance of Jesus' charge to the disciples in Matthew 10:40–42. Chapter 10 of Matthew's Gospel narrates the tradition of Jesus authorizing and commissioning the twelve disciples for mission. Jesus gave them power for the task of evangelism (10:1). The missionary discourse indicates that the disciples' ministry was an extension of Jesus' own ministry—they were heralds who were charged to proclaim the good news that in Jesus the dominion of heaven had come near (10:7). The good news of the coming of God's rule must be corroborated by concrete signs and demonstrations of God's care (10:8). Jesus restricted their mission to "the lost sheep of the house of Israel" (10:5–6), but the proclamation of God's rule would eventually extend to Gentiles (28:16–20).

Theses verses show that those who welcomed the twelve during their missionary tour welcomed Jesus and the One who sent Jesus. Extending hospitality to those who had likely experienced rejection, suffering, and even persecution (10:11–31) was exceedingly commendable (10:41).

Matthew's quotation of Jesus' words is instructive for his community. He reminds them that God is often present in exchanges between guests and their hosts. Hebrews 13:2 reiterates this theme: "Do not neglect to show hospitality to strangers, for by doing that some have entertained angels without knowing it."

Matthew's community knew that practicing the art of hospitality included sharing even small expressions of love and kindness with others. "Motive and not measure" could be a useful guideline for "there may be a sea of warm love in *a cup of cold water*."[2]

The refreshing and regenerating gift of cold water for the weary, thirsty traveler should not be taken for granted. Proverbs 25:25 captures this sentiment well: "Like cold water to a thirsty soul, so is good news from a far country."

Members of God's redeemed community, who are themselves recipients of God's welcoming and gracious hospitality, are to share the gifts, blessings, and bounty with which they have been blessed. Even "a cup of cold water" can function as a rich and meaningful symbol of the reality of boundless hospitality and the building of community among humankind.

Respond to the Word

- What can you and your community of faith do to be more hospitable to others?
- To whom will you show Christian hospitality this week? Consider serving in a soup kitchen or visiting one who is lonely.

Go with the Word

Hospitality for the Soul

It is worth some reflection to try to discern the patterns of this self-maintaining cycle of human suffering. For a person who feels unvalued, unappreciated, and goalless is not capable of generosity and appreciation of others and therefore, not capable of empathy and concern with their hunger and their need. In the strictest sense, such a person needs to be rescued, redeemed, or saved as much as the starving person whose quality of life is shriveled and brutalized needs to be rescued, redeemed, or saved. Both are living a life that is unfree, less than human, and marred by needless suffering. But the fearful frustration and torture of the physically starving person can only be resolved by that redemption of the love-starved which consists of a radical conversion from self-centeredness to engagement with and for others.

Monika Hellwig, *The Eucharist and the Hunger of the World* (New York: Paulist Press, 1976).

1. John Stambaugh, "Mobility and Mission." *The New Testament in Its Social Environment*, Wayne A. Meeks, ed. (Philadelphia: Westminster, 1986), 37–38.

2. Charles H. Spurgeon, *The King Has Come* (Old Tappan, N.J.: Fleming H. Revell, 1987), 132.

I Will Give You Rest

Come to me, all you that are weary and are carrying heavy burdens, and I will give you rest. Take my yoke upon you, and learn from me; for I am gentle and humble in heart, and you will find rest for your souls. For my yoke is easy, and my burden is light.

Matthew 11:28–30

Bible Reading   Matthew 11:16–19, 25–30

Additional Bible Readings: Genesis 24:34–38, 42–49, 58–67/
                                          Psalm 45:10–17
                                      or Song of Solomon 2:8–13
                                      or Zechariah 9:9–12/Psalm 145:8–14
                                      Romans 7:15–25a

Enter the Word

- Why is rest so important?
- How much real rest do you get?

Rest doesn't necessarily mean sleep. Some people find it restful to listen to quiet music or watch birds in the yard. Others find rest in a jigsaw puzzle or gardening.

Think about the last several weeks. Recall times when you felt rested and what you were doing at those times. Consider how you might build more times like that into your life.

There are many things in our lives that can be burdensome: being unemployed or underemployed, juggling too many responsibilities, caring for a sick family member, mourning the death of a loved one, moving, losing a close friend. Jesus knows what your burdens are—anything that makes you weary.

Think about, write down, or even tape record anything in your life that's bothering you, big or small. Envision yourself putting these burdens in a large sack. Or, literally place your list or cassette tape in a paper bag. Symbolically turn these burdens over to Jesus by putting the bag in a closet. Pray that Jesus will take these burdens, as he said he would. Then try to forget about them. In a few days open the bag and replay or reread your list. Identify the burdens you were able to release to Christ. Perhaps one or more of them have already been resolved.

Be sure to study today's additional readings from Genesis, Psalm 45 and 145, Song of Solomon, Zechariah, and Romans. Note how the Word of God brings you rest.

> *I am tired, and I am weary. Let me experience the rest that only you can give, Precious God. Amen.*

Engage the Word

- How are Jesus' words refreshing good news for Matthew's community of faith?

Jesus' amazing invitation in Matthew 11:28–30 presents a stirring snapshot of the boundless character of the gift of God's compassion.

Of immediate interest is that the tradition invites respondents to come to Jesus: "Come to me . . . I will give you rest" (Matthew 11:28). Verses 25–27 clarify why Jesus is qualified to provide life-refreshing rest: he has been authorized by God to do so.

The invitation to come is extended to "all" (11:28). There are no qualifiers citing privilege based on gender, racial, cultural, or national origin, age, economic status, or education. "All," *pantes*, who are weary or who carry heavy burdens of any kind may come to the One who gives rest. The good news for men and women in Matthew's community is that God's regenerative compassion is extended freely to all who ask.

The instructions to "take my yoke" and "learn from me" represent the second and third components of the threefold invitation

(11:29). As with the invitation for all to "come," respondents are provided yet another promise: "rest for your souls" (11:29c). Rest from the turmoil and turbulence of inward or external struggle will create the conditions in which true rest is possible.

The term "yoke," *zugon*, typically refers to a wooden or iron frame used on farm animals (e.g., oxen, 1 Samuel 6:7; 1 Kings 19:19; Luke 14:19). It could also mean "burdens" or "responsibilities" in a broader, figurative sense (Jeremiah 2:20, 5:5).

The summons to take Jesus' yoke upon one's self and learn from Jesus is found only in Matthew's Gospel. Matthew is highlighting an important point for his community: Jesus is the Teacher who shows women and men the way of God's righteousness (5:2). Matthew's Gospel contains five long blocks of Jesus' teaching material (chapters 5–7, 10, 13, 18, and 23–25). Although much of the content of the teaching material is found in the Gospel of Luke, Matthew alone organizes the material into separate, unified, didactic (teaching) discourses.

Matthew 11:28–30 shows that sitting at the feet of the One who helps Christians to chart the journey of life does not constitute tireless labor: it is actually the key to finding resplendent rest from the compassionate God. Jesus, who is "gentle and humble in heart" (11:29) will make God's compassion real to those who draw near.

One of the additional readings heralds the celebratory theme of the gift of God's compassion to humankind. In Psalm 145:9, the testimony to this dimension of God's character is clear: "God is good to all, and God's compassion is over all that God has made." May all realize the momentous significance of God's great compassion in their lives!

Respond to the Word

- How might your congregation organize its schedule of activities so as to underscore the importance of rest for all?
- What burden(s) will you lay before Jesus this week?

Go with the Word

The Rest Jesus Promises

The "rest" Jesus promises summons up the image of the escha-tological rest in the days of the Messiah, of which the sabbath rest was a symbol and a foretaste. Paradoxically, Jesus' "rest" was also a kind of "yoke," a symbol used by the rabbis for the Mosaic law. . . . Central to the yoke or law of Jesus . . . is Jesus himself. . . . The spiritual rest Jesus gives comes from assimilating and living Jesus' attitudes, indeed, his very person.

John P. Meier, *Matthew* (Wilmington, Del.: Michael Glazier, 1980), 148.

A Sower Went Out to Sow

And Jesus told them many things in parables, saying:

"Listen! A sower went out to sow."

Matthew 13:3

Bible Reading: Matthew 13:1–9, 18–23

Additional Bible Readings: Genesis 25:19–34/
                                            Psalm 119:105–112
                                            or Isaiah 55:10–13/
                                            Psalm 65:(1–8) 9–13
                                            Romans 8:1–11

Enter the Word

- What insights do Jesus' parables provide into God's dominion?
- In what ways are you a sower, especially of God's Word?

The parable of the sower in Matthew 13 tells how God's dominion can grow in the lives of those who receive the seeds of God's Word. In a poetic way it describes how a person might respond after God's seed is sown in the soil of his or her life. Jesus' words about seeds and soil may well describe two of the most important issues of our spiritual growth—the kind of soil we offer to God's seeds and the kinds of seeds we sow in Christ's name.

As you read Matthew 13:1–9, imagine yourself among the crowd. Look at the face of Jesus, who is standing in the boat. Perhaps Jesus is wondering who will really hear the words. Ask yourself how Jesus' words have meaning for you. Try to get a sense of actually hearing Jesus speaking from the boat. The first word he says is "Listen." Allow yourself to listen as Jesus speaks the parable.

Think about how your life is like one or more of the soils Jesus describes. Recall times when you were like each of these soils.

Accepting Jesus as Savior is the beginning of life lived in God's dominion. Through Christ, God has sown and we have accepted seeds of forgiveness, love, peace, justice, hope, and new life. Think about examples of these seeds in your life. Consider what kinds of seeds you sow in the garden of your life at home, at work, and at church. Think about ways the growth of your seeds affects the lives of other persons.

Read the explanation of the parable given in Matthew 13:18–23. Also read and reflect on this week's additional scriptures.

Sow in my heart seeds that yield a bountiful harvest.
Amen.

Engage the Word

- According to Matthew's Gospel, what does the parable of the sower teach the crowd and Jesus' disciples?

The parable of the sower has been called the "watershed" of Jesus' parables. All three Synoptic Gospels record the parable as the "introduction" to the collection of Jesus' subsequent parables (Mark 4:1–9; Luke 8:4–8; Matthew 13:1–9).

Jesus' parables represent a powerful and effective teaching medium. The parable traditions are usually comprised of short, narrative fiction, designed to effect a comparison of one thing to another. The central symbol in Jesus' parables is the "dominion of God." Drawing upon wide-ranging and familiar Palestinian symbols and imagery (seed, yeast, weeds, birds, a householder, a woman baking bread, light, a man with one hundred sheep, a woman with ten coins, and so forth), parables provide graphic and often colorful "word pictures" that unveil some dimension of the vision of God's rule in the world.

The parable of the sower is the flagship of the parables, deserving particular prominence. Jesus, the master storyteller, uses the agrarian imagery of the sowing of seed during planting season to teach a profoundly illuminating truth: the establishment of the rule of God's dominion is a "process." Like seed that has germinated, its potential for growth is a function of the collaboration of God's activity and human response. Human receptivity and response to the gospel can affect significantly both the process of growth and the nature of the yield, whether it will produce "some a hundred-fold, some sixty, some thirty" (Matthew 13:8).

Jesus clarifies the meaning of the parable for the disciples, leaving no doubt that the seed sown is God's dominion (13:18–19). Whether the seed fell on the path (and was devoured by birds, 13:4); on rocky ground (with little possibility of germination, and was scorched, 13:5–6); among thorns that choked them (13:7); or on good soil and produced a bountiful productive harvest (13:8), it is clear that both failure and the miracle of growth are within the realm of possible results. There may be loss, but there may be significant gain!

According to the writer of Matthew's Gospel, Jesus does not interpret the parable for the thronging, curious crowds; but, as noted above, he explains the meaning of the parable in "closed sessions" with the disciples. Declaring of the crowds, "The reason I speak to them in parables is that 'seeing they do not perceive, and hearing they do not understand' " (13:13), Jesus teaches a vital truth about human receptivity to the gospel: by submitting to God's reign, one can comprehend the mystery of Jesus' comparisons and may then understand and accept God's dominion. In this way, one is no longer a non-perceiving spectator but a disciple. Parables can assist in changing spectators into participants.

Psalm 119:105, one of the additional scriptures, attests that God's word is a "lamp" for the feet and a "light" for the path of God's people. Similarly, God's dominion in the parables provides light for members of Matthew's community as they journey through life in the world.

Respond to the Word

- How and where can you sow seeds of God's Word this week?
- What changes need to occur in the soil of your own life to increase the yield of God's Word?

Go with the Word

A Seed and a Sower

Christ told his parables in terms of things that never change in the barest fundamentals of living. And we can claim them for our own if we will make the effort to pierce the years with a little study, to breathe the clean air of the countryside and lift our eyes to the stars. . . . In a city park in London, in the sprawling mechanized farms of the American Middle West, in a backyard garden of a window box there is still a seed and a sower.

April Oursler Armstrong, *The Tales Christ Told*, adapted from Fulton
Oursler, *The Greatest Story Ever Told: The Life of Christ* (New York:
Doubleday, 1958), 9, 17, 18.

Wheat or Weeds?

Let both the wheat and weeds grow together until the harvest; and at harvest time I will tell the reapers, Collect the weeds first and bind them in bundles to be burned, but gather the wheat into my barn.

Matthew 13:30

Bible Reading: Matthew 13:24–30, 36–43

Additional Bible Readings: Genesis 28:10–19a/
                                      Psalm 139:1–12, 23–24
                                   or Isaiah 44:6–8/Psalm 86:11–17
                                   Romans 8:12–25

Enter the Word

- For what reasons is wheat preferable to weeds?
- What might the distinction between these two plants suggest to you about the dominion of God?

The parable of the wheat and the weeds offers a way to think about our individual spiritual lives as well as the assurance of God's judgment of good and evil. Matthew 13:41 promises that God's angels will remove "all causes of sin and all evildoers." Jesus names the good seed "children of God's dominion" and the bad seed "children of the evil one" (13:38). Our individual thoughts and actions may be either! A person may ask, "What kinds of seeds am I sowing in my own life and in the lives of other persons?"

Invite the Spirit of Christ to guide you as you read Matthew 13:24–30. Allow your imagination to create an impression of wheat and weeds growing together. Let yourself watch them grow until harvest. Observe as the wheat is gathered and placed in the barn. Watch as the weeds are tied into bundles and burned. Pay attention to any thoughts or feelings you may have.

First identify feelings, thoughts, and actions in your life that are good seed. Then identify feelings, thoughts, and actions in your life that are bad seed. You may wish to list these on paper. Think about ways God's judgment may offer hope to you as both good and bad seed grow together in your life.

Life does not always seem fair. People who do good sometimes suffer. People who do harm sometimes seem to have good fortune. Think of these situations in your life. Consider ways the parable of the wheat and the weeds might offer hope in these situations.

Now read Matthew 13:36–43. Be alert for insights into the meaning of Jesus' parable that you may have missed. See if you can restate the parable and its meaning in two or three sentences.

Continue your Bible study by reading the passages from Genesis, Psalm 139 and 86, Isaiah, and Romans.

> I confess that my life shows forth weeds as well as wheat. Help me to pull up the weeds so that the wheat may flourish. Amen.

Engage the Word

- What might this parable have taught Matthew's community about themselves in relation to God's dominion?

The parable of the wheat and weeds, found only in Matthew's Gospel, teaches an important lesson: wheat (the children of God's dominion) and weeds (the children of the evil one) will grow together until the close of human history (Matthew 13:36–43).

The writer of Matthew's Gospel compares the dominion of God's rule to a landed proprietor who discovers that his field is full of bothersome weeds. Customarily, workers would gather the weeds so that they could be dried and used for fuel (wood was scarce in Palestine). But the extraction of the plentiful weeds could damage the tender wheat plants. This is the case for two reasons. First, in the early stages, the wheat and weeds were sometimes indistinguishable. Second, the stronger roots of the weeds could damage the roots of the wheat. The landowner allows the wheat and the weeds to grow together, undisturbed, until the time of harvest.

The "field" represents the world (13:38). The "end of the age" will thus be a time of judgment for the world, with contrasting fates for the evildoers ("[God's angels] will throw them into the furnace of fire," 13:42) and the righteous ("the righteous will shine like the sun in the dominion of God's rule," 13:43).

The parable illustrates the landowner's (God's) patience: "Let both [the wheat and weeds] grow together until the harvest" (13:30). Moreover, it is clear that God alone will determine the qualitative difference between the wheat and the weeds. Human judgment is not invoked. Until harvest time, then, the church will include a mixture of both "true disciples" and "pseudo-disciples."

For the writer of Matthew's Gospel, the parable of the wheat and the weeds can function to remind members of Matthew's community that even if God's harvest (a time of judgment) is coming, the opportunity to live fully as "good seed" ("the children of God's dominion," 13:38) is not yet past. Persons who live in the dominion of God's rule are to persevere as followers of God's way. Further, the church will be a *corpus mixtum*, a "mixed body" of saints and sinners, the righteous and the unrighteous, until the harvest. Church members are not to make premature judgment about who is "in" (wheat) and who is "out" (weeds).

A motif citing the need for humankind to engage in self-examination of life before God (for God alone knows all human hearts) is presented in Psalm 139:23–24. The writer (likely David) says that all who seek to live in the light of God's rule must allow God to conduct the innermost search of the heart—a requisite step for growth in the knowledge and ways of God. Only God can lead the trusting one into the ways of righteousness.

Respond to the Word

- How might this parable help your congregation to be more inclusive and less judgmental?
- What weeds will you ask God to uproot in your own life?

Go with the Word

The Touch of Mercy

Mr. Head stood very still and felt the action of mercy touch him again but this time he knew that there were no words in the world that could name it. He understood that it grew out of agony, which is not denied to any man and which is given in strange ways to children. He understood it was all a man could carry into death to give his Maker and he suddenly burned with shame that he had so little of it to take with him. He stood appalled, judging himself with the thoroughness of God, while the action of mercy covered his pride like a flame and consumed it. He had never thought himself a great sinner before but he saw now that his true depravity had been hidden from him lest it cause him despair. He realized that he was forgiven for sins from the beginning of time, when he had conceived in his own heart the sin of Adam, until the present, when he had denied poor Nelson. He saw that no sin was too monstrous for him to claim as his own, and since God loved in proportion as [God] forgave, he felt ready at that instant to enter Paradise.

Flannery O'Connor, "The Artificial Nigger," in *Flannery O'Connor: The Complete Stories* (New York: Farrar, Straus & Giroux, 1979), 269–70.

Parables of God's Dominion

"The dominion of heaven is like . . . "

Matthew 13:33a

Bible Reading: Matthew 13:31–33, 44–52

Additional Bible Readings: Genesis 29:15–28/
                                        Psalm 105:1–11, 45b
                                        (or Psalm 128)
                                        or 1 Kings 3:5–12/
                                        Psalm 119:129–136
                                        Romans 8:26–39

Enter the Word

- What are some of the stories, art, music, and poetry that help you envision God's dominion?
- What do you think God's dominion is like?

Read Matthew 13:31–32. Imagine a tiny seed growing into a large plant. Picture the growth as it happens. Watch the birds flying in and out of the branches. See the nests. In your own life consider which God-given qualities grow like the plant. Name the life situations that indicate the growth of these qualities. Think about what the birds might represent in your life. Consider how the growth of your God-given qualities provides nesting places for these birds.

Read Matthew 13:33. Imagine the woman mixing the yeast into the dough. Observe as she kneads the bread. See how she shapes the loaves of bread. Watch the loaves of bread rise. Think about how her work helps the bread rise. Reflect on ways God might be working in your life to help you grow in God's dominion.

Read Matthew 13:44–46. Name the old and new "treasures" in your life. Consider the treasures of God's dominion. Reflect on your willingness to give all you have in order to experience the fullness of God's dominion in your life.

As you read Matthew 13:47–52 picture how God's dominion is like a dragnet. Imagine the coming judgment and how God will see you when this net is dragged ashore.

Read the additional scriptures and ponder what these passages have to say about God's dominion.

> *Knead my heart, God, so that my faith will increase and my actions will point others toward you. Amen.*

Engage the Word

- What conclusions about the dominion of God might Matthew's community have drawn from these parables?

Matthew 13:31–33, 44–52, introduces a collection of five parables, often called parables of growth. The parables shed important light on the nature of God's dominion, illustrating the sharp discrepancy between the "hiddenness" of God's dominion at its initial sowing and the significantly expansive potential of its final fruition. The parables invite faith in the God who continues to act in the ministry of Jesus.

The first two parables, the parable of the mustard seed and the parable of the yeast, are addressed to the "great crowds" gathered about Jesus as he sat in a boat near the sea (Matthew 13:2, 31–36a). The parables of the treasure hidden in a field, the merchant in search of fine pearls, and the net thrown into the sea (13:44–52) are addressed to the disciples (13:36, 51).

The parable of the mustard seed is a particularly fitting story to describe the nature of God's dominion in the world. The mustard seed, the tiniest of Palestinian seeds that was visible to the naked eye, would grow into a mustard plant 8 to 12 feet high. Matthew emphasizes that this "greatest of shrubs" (13:32) has branches that sustain the nests of the birds of the air. The dominion of God, like the mustard seed, progresses from seemingly negligible beginnings to a dominion that all the world can see.

The parable of the yeast makes a similar point about successful fruition. Yeast, of seemingly negligible worth in its original form, promotes significant growth in flour. Yeast mixed with three measures of flour would produce a quantity of bread large enough to feed a great number of people.

In scripture, yeast has sometimes functioned as a symbol of the corrupt effects of evil. Exodus 34:18 prohibits the use of leavened bread in sacrifices. Jesus issues a warning to the disciples to guard against the "yeast of the Pharisees and Sadducees" (Matthew 16:6, 11f; but note that in Mark 8:15 it is "the yeast of the Pharisees and the yeast of Herod"). Sometimes yeast is associated with that which is good (Leviticus 7:13–14; 23:17). For Matthew, yeast in rising flour is an appropriate symbol to illustrate the potential magnitude of the growth of God's dominion in the world.

Matthew 13:44–52 contains three parables addressed specifically to the disciples. All stress human response to God's activity. The parables of the treasure hidden in a field and the merchant in search of fine pearls (13:44–45) together show that one who discovers the marvelous realities of the dominion of heaven is willing to make great sacrifices to obtain it.

The parable of the net thrown into the sea concerns future judgment. Whether the "net" refers to the "church" with its mixed composition of persons, or to the "whole world" with both repentant and unrepentant persons mixed together (an evangelistic interest may be present in the latter option), God's angels will separate the righteous from the evil. Sorting is God's business.

The five parables together illustrate some aspect of the character of the dominion of God's rule. Members of Matthew's community can affirm together that the mosaic of God's wondrous plan of salvation for humankind is rich indeed.

Respond to the Word

- How can you and your congregation live out the meaning of these parables so that others may imagine the dominion of God?
- What are you willing to do to experience the dominion of God?

Go with the Word

O give thanks to God.
Call on God's name.
Tell the people what God has done.
The unfolding of God's words
    gives light and understanding to all people.
Sing to God! Sing praises to God!
Tell of all God's wonderful works!
May God's face shine on us all and teach us God's ways.
Glory in God's name.
Let the hearts of all who seek God rejoice.

The Inviting Word Youth Learner's Guide (Cleveland, Ohio: United
Church Press, 1995), 104. Used by permission.

Face-to-Face Encounter

Jacob was left alone; and a man wrestled with him until daybreak. So Jacob called the place Peniel, saying, "For I have seen God face to face and yet my life is preserved."

Genesis 32:24, 30

Bible Reading:	Genesis 32:22–31
Additional Bible Readings:	Psalm 17:1–7, 15
	or Isaiah 55:1–5/
	Psalm 145:8–9, 14–21
	Romans 9:1–5
	Matthew 14:13–21

Enter the Word

- What might a face-to-face encounter with God be like?
- How would you describe your own encounter(s) with God?

Find a time and place where you can be completely alone. If possible, let this be at night. Once you are comfortably seated and relaxed, reflect on a time when your relationship with God involved conflict or struggle. If it involved an event or experience that seemed meaningless at the moment, recall how you made sense of the situation. Ponder what caused you to wrestle with your faith. Identify the roles others played in your crisis or turmoil. Recollect your sense of where God was during this event.

Try to remember how that situation *felt* inside of you. Explain

226

how the struggle was resolved and at what cost. Describe the changes in you and/or your faith that resulted.

Before reading the text, call to mind the story of Jacob and Esau (Genesis 27:1–28:5) and of how Jacob tricked his brother, first out of his birthright with a bowl of lentil stew, then out of the elder son's blessing by father Isaac with a disguise. Imagine how Jacob might feel years later about returning to meet Esau. Ask yourself what would weigh on Jacob's mind and heart.

Read Genesis 32:22–31 aloud, one verse at a time. Pause between each verse to *view* the unfolding picture from the perspectives of Jacob, of the stranger, of the family waiting across the Jabbok.

Reflect on how Jacob's struggle compares with your own. Ponder whatever qualities you have in common with Jacob—wrestlings, blessings, new identities, "limpings."

Now read the additional scriptures. Isaiah 55 looks ahead to a time when the people held captive in Babylon will be restored to Israel. In Romans, Paul struggles with his desire that all of Israel would come to know Christ. Jesus fed five thousand listeners in Matthew 14. Psalm 17 is a prayer for deliverance, whereas Psalm 145 lifts up the character of God.

> *I want to encounter you and yet I don't, Mighty God, because such meetings lead to struggle and transformation. Amen.*

Engage the Word

- How is Jacob's struggle with the angel a model for all who encounter God?

It is no accident that Jacob's name means "he who supplants." According to the Bible, he struggled with his brother Esau from before their birth in the womb of their mother Rebekah (Genesis 25:22–26). Jacob, who was born a few seconds later than his brother Esau and who wanted to be the elder heir of his father Isaac, would obtain Esau's birthright (25:27–34). Jacob later deceived their father so as to get his final blessing, which rightfully belonged to Esau (Genesis 27). As a result Esau planned to kill Jacob, prompting Jacob to flee to Haran, where he remained for twenty years (27:41–45; 31:41).

Genesis 32 narrates the story of Jacob's reconciliation with Esau. Fearing danger from Esau and his four-hundred person entourage who were approaching him (32:1–8), Jacob prayerfully committed his life into God's hands (32:9–12) and shrewdly used his wealth to gain favor in the eyes of his estranged brother (32:13–21).

Genesis 32:22–31 narrates the account of Jacob's face-to-face encounter with God. An anxious and contrite Jacob had already prayed for protection from the God who had shown steadfast love and faithfulness (32:9–12). Now God appears in the form of a nocturnal visitor and wrestles all night with Jacob, concluding the struggle only at daybreak (32:24–26).

Alone with God, Jacob learned that prayer, a face-to-face encounter with God, may involve a depth of intimacy with God that includes great—and even painful—struggle. At the end of his own resources, and likely facing overwhelming feelings of fear, anguish, despair, and vulnerability, Jacob tarried long with God, fully open to divine intervention and determined to obtain some indication of God's blessing (32:26–29).

Jacob called the place of intimacy and consuming struggle with God "Peniel" (32:30). Peniel became a symbol of the reality that his strength and transformation came from prayerful surrender and perseverance in a face-to-face encounter with a gracious God.

Psalm 17, one of the additional scripture passages, is a prayer for deliverance from enemies. It mirrors many of the concerns in Genesis 32:22–21. Chief among them, and instructive for all who recognize the inevitability of the need for intimacy with God through prayer, is the testimony to God's steadfast love in the light of the recognition of human limitation. Like both Jacob and the psalmist, women and men will find a God who hears in the time of need.

Respond to the Word

- How can you, perhaps along with others, support those who are struggling with God?
- As you identify the dark places where you struggle in your own life, what action will you allow God to take to transform you?

Go with the Word

Changed by God

Both were wounded: Jacob at the hip, the angel in his vanity. Yet they parted friends, or was it accomplices? Jacob accepted his aggressor's departure willingly; the latter, as if to thank him, made him a gift: a new name which for generations to come would symbolize eternal struggle and endurance, in more than one land, during more than one night.

At dawn Jacob was a different man. Whatever he touched caught fire. His words acquired a new resonance; he now expressed himself as a visionary, a poet.

Elie Wiesel, *Messengers of God: Biblical Portraits and Legends* (New York: Random House, 1976), 94.

You of Little Faith

Jesus said, "Come." So Peter got out of the boat, started walking on the water, and came toward Jesus. But when he noticed the strong wind, he became frightened, and beginning to sink cried out, "Lord, save me!" Jesus immediately reached out his hand and caught Peter saying to him, "You of little faith, why did you doubt?"

Matthew 14:29–31

Bible Reading: Matthew 14:22–33

Additional Bible Readings: Genesis 37:1–4, 12–28/
                                 Psalm 105:1–6, 16–22, 45b
                       or 1 Kings 19:9–18/
                                 Psalm 85:8–13
                       Romans 10:5–15

Enter the Word

- What does it mean to have faith?
- What might Jesus say to you about your faith?

Jesus understood the need to be replenished. He often went off by himself to pray so that he would be ready to meet the needs of the masses. Think about the activities in your life. Perhaps you can attribute negative feelings to fatigue or stress. Think of ways you might adjust your schedule to include rest and prayer.

Read Matthew 14:22–33. Envision Jesus walking on the water.

Imagine how the disciples must have felt as they watched him. Consider Peter's thoughts as he got out of the boat. Ponder Jesus' compassionate response to his frightened friends. Think about a time when you have felt as though you were in a boat battered by high winds. Imagine Jesus speaking to you and calming the chaos. Consider your own response to the presence and power of Christ in the stormy places of your life.

As long as Peter's focus was on Jesus, he walked. When his focus was on the wind, his fear returned and he began to sink. Jesus' first action was to reach out to Peter and save him. Then he commented on Peter's faith: "You of little faith, why did you doubt?" (Matthew 14:31). Think about a time when you experienced Christ lifting you as you seemed to be sinking in the waves. Jesus' words remind us of God's saving presence, even when our fear interferes with the empowering energy of faith.

Read the additional scriptures and ponder their meaning.

> *Just as you beckoned to Peter, help me to take a leap of faith when the storms of life threaten me. Amen.*

Engage the Word

* How might the story of Jesus walking on the water have helped Matthew's community recognize the relationship among fear, doubt, and trust?

Religious writers have long lauded Matthew 14:22–33 as an inspirational testament to the reality of human doubt and Jesus' mighty power to save.

The tradition of Jesus walking on the water is narrated in three gospels (Matthew 14:22–33; Mark 6:45–52; and John 6:16–21), but it is in Matthew's Gospel alone that we find the account of Peter's voluntary excursion from the security of the boat to walk toward Jesus on the sea. The other disciples, who had been battling the tumultuous waves, remained in the boat (Matthew 14:24–26).

Of immediate significance in Peter's experience with fear and doubt is the "wind." Fierce winds precipitated the disciples' struggle in the boat (Matthew 14:24). The wind was the cause of Peter's fear: "But when he noticed the strong wind, he became frightened"

(14:30). The ceasing of the wind corroborated Jesus' sovereignty over all nature (14:32–33).

Peter's willingness to engage in the risk-taking of faith, even with Divine authorization ("Jesus said, 'Come,' " 14:29), failed for one simple reason: he took his eyes off Jesus (14:30a). When Peter lost sight of Jesus, he became overwhelmed by the difficult circumstances before him. Peter's experience thus highlights a very important truth: the origin of "little faith" and doubt is not always a lack of understanding or necessarily attributable to disbelief. Trust often falters due to "fear"; and if in addition to fear the eyes of the heart are shifted away from God, "little faith" is an inevitable result.

Peter's prayerful cry, "Lord, save me!" (14:30), was short, but it brought a renewed focus on Jesus. Jesus restored Peter (14:31).

Matthew's readers can derive great comfort from this story. When fear gives way to "little faith" and the focus is more on the surrounding "waves" of danger and crisis instead of God, then Jesus, Emmanuel ("God-with-us"), is present (1:23). The English words "It is I" (14:27) are translated literally from the Greek as "I am" (see Exodus 3:14). God endowed Jesus with supernatural power (28:18). Jesus stands ready to provide saving help.

First Kings 19:9–18, one of additional scriptures for today, narrates the story of Elijah's experience with fear and doubt. He had just garnered a great victory against the priests of Baal on Mt. Carmel, demonstrating that the God of Israel was triumphant over the gods of Baal (1 Kings 18:1–46). But when he learned that Jezebel sought his life, his dejection and fear was almost "unto death" (19:4). Following the instructions of the angel who later appears to him, Elijah traveled to Horeb, the "mount of God," (19:8); there he experienced renewal in the presence of the God who was near. He learned that even if "little faith" is at times a very real part of human experience, it need not be the last word for the people of God.

Respond to the Word

- How can you help someone who is doubtful or fearful to strengthen his or her faith and place greater trust in God?
- What fears and doubts will you bring to Christ this week?

Go with the Word

Empowered to Care

Jesus' miracle of walking on the sea is not just to "show off" who he is but to come to the aid of his threatened disciples. That is to say, while the story is indeed talking about who Jesus is, it emphasizes his *function* rather than his *nature*. As Messiah he is the one charged and empowered by God to shepherd and care for God's people.

Douglas R.A. Hare, *Matthew: Interpretation, A Bible Commentary for Teaching and Preaching* (Louisville: John Knox, 1993), 169.

Life Together

How very good and pleasant it is when kindred live together in unity!

Psalm 133:1

Bible Reading:	Psalm 133
Additional Bible Readings:	Genesis 45:1–15
	or Isaiah 56:1, 6–8/Psalm 67
	Romans 11:1–2a, 29–32
	Matthew 15:(10–20) 21–28

Engage the Word

- What are the marks of a life that is good, pleasant, and lived in unity?
- How would you describe your own experience among God's people?

Read Psalm 133. The phrase "live together in unity" suggests a great deal more than to simply "live together." We are together on the earth in our various geographical locations—our towns, our nations, and our world. We share time and space with one another. We are more alike than we are different. The hopes, fears, and dreams of each of us are probably very similar. It makes sense to create goodness and pleasantness by identifying specific ways to live together in unity.

Close your eyes, relax, and remember a pleasant time you have had with a group of people, perhaps family, friends, or co-workers. Think about what you were doing, who was there, and what kinds of feelings you had. Imagine that you are creating an event in the future that will help everyone experience those good feelings once again. Think about what everyone is doing, who the people are, and where you are located. Fill in all the details in your imagination.

Consider other small ways you might "live together in unity" with people you know and see daily. Perhaps you might write someone a letter, make a phone call, or just listen to someone who needs to talk. Consider doing one of those things this week.

Think about the relationships you have with members of your family. Make a mental note of the things that you might do to make the relationships "good and pleasant."

As you read the additional scriptures, be aware of ideas in them that may help you live in unity with others.

> *Let me live in unity with others, O God, so that life may be good and pleasant as you intended. Amen.*

Engage the Word

- What are some of the ways Psalm 133 may have been interpreted and understood?

Psalm 133 is one of the shortest psalms, but its brevity does not mask its inviting imagery of familial joyousness and inclusive unity.

Some interpreters suggest that the psalmist is praising the ancient Israelite practice of brothers living together (even when they are married; see Deuteronomy 25:5–10). Still others suggest that this psalm has its origins in a particular historical episode, such as Nehemiah's attempt to repopulate Jerusalem, noting that it presented a lofty ideal of unity to be aimed at the new community.[1]

A broader and widely accepted context of Psalm 133 suggests that it depicts a pilgrimage to Jerusalem. Like other songs of ascents, it highlights the covenant communion of the pilgrims in Jerusalem.

Whatever the precise historical context of Psalm 133 might be, its crowning emphasis on the benefit of life together among God's people is unmistakable. The psalmist declares that such unity is not just good, but "very good," and it is equally "pleasant" (133:1).

Given the historical context, it is highly unlikely that the phrase "live together in unity" should necessarily be taken literally, as if a family (or members of an extended family) lived together under one roof (although, unity and solidarity among those bonded by kinship ties is desirable). Far more plausible is the likelihood that the psalmist is celebrating the spiritual and familial unity of God's people.

The clear allusions to precious oil "running down" and "running over" Aaron's beard and priestly collar, respectively (Psalm 133:2), may evoke thoughts of the descent of divine blessing upon a community united in God's love.

The image of the unity of God's people is compared to "the dew of Hermon which falls on the mountains of Zion" (133:3). The phrase "dew of Hermon" was a proverbial expression for "heavy dew." Dew, a visible entity, is water from the air condensed on a cool surface (in this case, the mountains of Zion). Dew would provide refreshing nourishment for the plants that needed to survive the hot Palestinian climate during the dry months (there was almost no rainfall from May to August). The presence of dew thus represents blessed relief from a harsh external environment and the promise of fruitfulness. In a similar manner, the unity of God's people provides life-giving nourishment and salutary benefits for life.

One of the additional scriptures for today illustrates the blessedness of familial tranquillity. The moving account of Joseph's reconciliation with his brothers in Genesis 45:1–15 illustrates yet another dimension of the effects of true cohesiveness in a community that places a premium on unity and growth together. Truly, how very good and pleasant it is when kindred live together in joyous communion!

Respond to the Word

- What change could you help your church, workplace, or community make so that people will interact more pleasantly?
- What could you do to create greater unity among your family?

Go with the Word

God of All

> *God of all, source and goal of community,*
> *whose will it is that all your people enjoy*
> *fullness of life, may we be builders*
> *of community, caring for your good earth*
> *here and worldwide, that we may delight*
> *in diversity and choose solidarity, for you are*
> *in community with us, our God, forever.*
> *Amen.*

Anonymous prayer

1. A. A. Anderson, *The Book of Psalms*, volume 2, The New Century Bible (London: Oliphants, 1972), 885.

We, Who Are Many—One Body

We, who are many, are one body in Christ, and individually we are members one of another.

Romans 12:5

Bible Reading:	Romans 12:1–8
Additional Bible Readings:	Exodus 1:8–2:10/Psalm 124
	or Isaiah 51:1–6/Psalm 138
	Matthew 16:13–20

Enter the Word

- How might "unity among diversity" describe the church?
- What gifts do you have to contribute to Christ's body?

Read Romans 12:1–8. Paul calls believers to offer themselves as a living sacrifice to God. The call is for people to go beyond themselves and their individual boundaries into a life that is within the body of Christ.

Just as Paul summoned the early Christians into service, his words still call believers to recognize themselves and others as part of the corporate body of Christ. We each have at least one special gift to bring in service to Christ. We are called to use that gift.

Name your gifts. Write down things you do well. Think about the people you know in your church. Consider what things they do well. Think about the ways your church benefits from a variety of talents and skills given by different people. Imagine what the life of your church would be like if all the members had the same gift.

How lucky we are that we are able to share the gifts that each of us brings to worship and the congregational life. The voices of the choir members, the dedication and insights of the Bible study leaders, and the openness of the children all enrich the lives of others. The family of God is filled with unique and different people. Think about the lives, talents, and gifts of those people that you know and thank God for their contributions.

Exodus 1:8–2:10 speaks of Israel's bondage in Egypt and sets the stage for God's call of Moses, a gifted leader. Psalm 138 is a prayer for deliverance from enemies, whereas Psalm 124 gives thanks for God's salvation from foes. Isaiah 51 points back to Israel's heritage and ahead to God's salvation of the people. In Matthew 16, Peter confesses that Jesus is the Messiah.

> *Thank you, God, for the diverse gifts each one of us is able to give to edify the body of Christ. Amen.*

Engage the Word

- How might Paul's words have helped the church deal with the problems that diversity of gifts may bring?

Paul addressed a problem in Romans 12:1–8 that was probably experienced in several first-century churches; that is, the problem of the use of one's gifts for Christian ministry and service. Paul shows that a diversity of individual gifts enriches the life of the Christian community.

Some Roman Christians were "overrating" their gifts, thinking more highly of themselves than they ought (Romans 12:3). Others may have tended to "underrate" the importance of some of the gifts as of lesser consequence, so Paul seeks to impart a balanced perspective that will benefit the entire community (12:4–6a). There are no "negligible" gifts of the Spirit in the body.

Paul enjoins his readers to "think with sober judgment, each according to the measure of faith that God has assigned" (12:3b). The Greek word for "sober judgment," *sophronein*, denotes modesty or moderation, restraint, and discretion.

Paul's repeated correlation of the "oneness" of the body with the "diversity" of its members in verses 3–8 underscores a fundamental reality of the church: the body is not one "despite" its diversity, but it is one body *by virtue of* its diversity. (The phrase "one body" occurs in verses 4–5, and verse 5 reiterates that "we who are many are one body in Christ.") That is, if there were not diversity in the body and all members were the same or nearly the same, the body would be a nearly unrecognizable, non-functional entity (1 Corinthians 12:17–20).

Paul's discussion of the wonderful diversity of those in the one body in 1 Corinthians 12:14–18, 20, is appropriate to share within this context:

> *Indeed, the body does not consist of one member but of many. If the foot would say, "Because I am not a hand, I do not belong to the body," that would not make it any less a part of the body. And if the ear would say, "Because I am not an eye, I do not belong to the body," that would not make it any less a part of the body. If the whole body were an eye, where would the hearing be? If the whole body were hearing, where would the sense of smell be? But as it is, God arranged the members in the body, each one of them, as God chose. . . . As it is, there are many members, yet one body.*

The diversity of individual gifts in the Christian community is an expression of the multifaceted abundance of God's grace. A rich plurality of gifts given to the many in one body is to be exercised and shared in ways that promote the health, nurture, well-being, and transformation of the whole.

Of greatest consequence to Paul is that all who are in the Christian community are "members of one another" (Romans 12:5). His witness to the insoluble interdependence of women and men in the one body nullifies the option of all striving for autonomy, and it confirms that diversity is vital for its healthy functioning.

Respond to the Word

- Whose gifts will you affirm this week? How can you do that?
- Which of your gifts do you need to offer to God's people? How will you do that?

Go with the Word

God of Change and Glory

God of change and glory, God of time and space,
when we fear the future, give to us your grace.
In the midst of changing ways, give us still the grace to praise.

God of many colors, God of many signs,
you have made us different, blessing many kinds.
As the old ways disappear, let your love cast out our fear.

Freshness of the morning, newness of each night,
you are still creating endless love and light.
This we see, as shadows part, many gifts from one great heart.

Many gifts, one Spirit, one love known in many ways.
In our difference is blessing, from diversity we praise
one Giver, one Word, one Spirit, one God
known in many ways, hallowing our days.
For the Giver, for the gifts, praise, praise, praise!

Index of Scriptures

Hebrew Scriptures

Gospels

Epistles and Other New Testament Scriptures